BAD LANGUAGE

A catalogue record for this book is available
from the British Library.

400 Kingsland Road
London
E8 4AA
peninsulapress.co.uk

Cover design by David Pearson

Typesetting by Geethik Technologies

Printed in Great Britain by CPI Group (UK) Ltd, Croydon

2 4 6 8 10 9 7 5 3 1

ISBN-13: 9781913512798

Epigraph from 'Adam's Law', from *Adam* by Gboyega Odubanjo is
quoted with the permission of the Estate of Gboyega Odubanjo
and Faber and Faber Ltd.

Epigraph from 'Dragonfly' from *The Books of Earthsea* by
Ursula K. Le Guin is quoted by permission of Theo Downes-Le Guin.

BAD LANGUAGE

SO MAYER

PENINSULA PRESS, LONDON

for the niblings,
who might be going to have read this a long,
long time from now.

and let us think say   for the reference therein   to the veritable
                                                                      bugaboo
the english language must be pooh pooh-ed quod erat
                                                        demonstrandum
          reh teh teh
— Gboyega Odubanjo, 'Adam's Law,' *Adam*

'I could chase an etymology on the brink of doom...
          [and] that's where we are... What comes next?'...
'Change, change,' said the Patterner. 'Transformation.'
— Ursula K. Le Guin, 'Dragonfly', *Tales from Earthsea*

CONTENTS

INHALE

There is no such thing as a safe word.

Safe comes from the Latin word salvus, meaning saved or secure. It first appears in written English around 1300, in the Christian sense of salvation. Within twenty-five years, it comes to mean physically rather than spiritually well, and thus free from danger. It sprouts a noun, meaning a secure place, particularly for storing coins and documents, about a hundred years later: from the soul to money in a century.

As poet Nam Le writes, because of 'the philological violence *within* language... a dictionary is a site of massacre'. There are no safe words, and that is why I wrote this book. There are no safe words, that is, unless we explore and examine and expand them together, to stake a collective claim to mutual meaning-making, or what – by expanding words – we could call mutual (s)aid. This is a practice I learned through queer BDSM, precisely through the negotiation and affirmation of what is called a safe word: a word that is specific and provisional to a given scene or configuration of people and occasion. It has to be mutually selected and mutually comprehensible, and is both consented to and used as a demonstration that consent is an ongoing practice, not a fixed contract.

It's not the semantic content of a word that makes it safe in BDSM. In fact, a safe word is often selected for its rarity, and for being easy to enunciate clearly: inescapably itself not semantically but sonically, a word you are otherwise unlikely to use in the situation, and that does not sound like anything but itself (it would be bad to use but as a safe word, for example). The pleasure of the queer practice of safe words draws our attention to the qualities of verbal language that are most neglected in Eurowestern (henceforth EW, for obvious reasons) culture: sounds, and the orifices that produce them. Sound and fury signify. Beyond the sonic and evocative qualities of the verbal, words are – even in writing – given full meaning by breath, gesture, micro-movement, accent and dozens more embodied modes. Not just consonants but also consonance: sounding-together.

In talking about language, and particularly about verbal language, I am conscious of a default assumption that everyone is hearing, and hearing in the same way. Yet in their very long history, oracy and listening have flexibly encompassed multiple non-hearing practices, including signing, sight, and both vibrational and direct touch. In conversation with Judith Butler in the film *Examined Life* (Astra Taylor, 2008), artist and disability justice activist Sunaura Taylor affirms that she goes for walks in her wheelchair; walking is her term for the pleasurable activity of traversing space at a self-managed pace that allows for sensory attention. So, I am re-meaning listening as a multi-sensory practice, in parallel with Taylor's redefinition of walking.

Despite their sight rhyme, lis-ten does not share a root with at-ten-d, but if we let them come together then perhaps listend, as a hybrid word, can engage us in attending beyond standard ableist taxonomies of senses and their capacities. If we are listending, then everything is articulating.

Listend, then, with your whole body through salvus. Beyond the Latin word you can just hear its Greek root: holos/houlos. Whole, holistic. The word holistic has become associated with the wellness-industrial complex, but it means nothing more or less than whole – not in the sense of a monolith, but a whole that is made up of interconnected parts, as language is. As a rootless cosmopolitan, I root around for wholeness in language, in order to root myself therein. Yet I am arrested by philological violence, over and over, and that motivates me to continue my protest action, my escape: to dig with intent using the very same weapons, which are words; to blunt and remake them through usage. The *Oxford English Dictionary* (*OED*) is my frenemesis. It is my go-to when a word gets me going. Like God, it is both immense in scope and infinite in detail. And, like the monotheistic God, it claims to be the be-all and end-all, so yes, when it comes to making meaning, I have an OEDipus complex. For all its big dictionary energy, it is but the tip of the linguistic iceberg. Insisting that only written records count towards establishing etymologies and usages, it misses the vast corpus of everyday usage preceding, exceeding and refusing official print, particularly spoken language whose trace is in the memories and bodies of its users. I'll take the orificial over the official every time. We cannot resign from dominance languages, but we can re-sign them.

We make ourselves up. It seems like a circular phrase, a closed repetition, but it is not. Introducing her anthology of writing by feminists of colour *Making Face, Making Soul / Haciendo Caras*, Gloria Anzaldúa writes:

> 'Making faces' is my metaphor for constructing one's identity. '[U]sted es el modeador de su carne tanto como el de su alma.' You are the shaper of your flesh as well as of your soul. According to the ancient nahuas, one was put on earth to create one's 'face' (body) and 'heart' (soul). To them, the soul was a speaker of words and the body a doer of deeds.

The English verbal phrase to make up has a dizzying range of meanings that echo the Greek word poeisis, making, the root of the English word poetry: everything from a face to a story to a table to a friendship to a world can be made up. To make (oneself) up means reckoning with the relation between deeds and words, and with what is made up by speaking.

'To make up' is a transitive verb, which is one that requires an object. I make up a character or a bed; and yet, after an argument, we make up. In the former example, make up takes an object; in the latter, make up omits its object, and so appears to be intransitive. For a verb to be able to do both is known as ambitransitivity. Ambi- (also written umbe- and amphi-, as in amphitheatre) can mean around or encompassing; it can also mean going both ways. Ambi as in ambivalent, ambiguous, ambitious, which is how I am for language, as an ambisexual ambigendered person. I want language, like me, to contain multitudes. Ambiguity is generative because it asks us to listen and negotiate meaning between us. If I say 'we made up', it's a complete sentence; as an ambitransitive usage, it could suggest that we repair our relationship by imagining and crafting together. Making up is both ambitransitive and holistic, a way of reconnecting both concepts and beings.

When we make up, we might be composing (a poem, song, story, self, lewk, relationship) – but we are also composting. We do not make up anything, including ourselves, out of nothing, but from roots and remains. Compose, compost and composit, the old art of laying out a book in hot type, all grow from the same Latin root: the verb componere, meaning to put or place together. We make ourselves up together out of what we have.

Often, what we have is not what we want. Like the English language, our histories may be haunted houses, and re-entering them can be unsettling. An exorcism in the

14

Catholic tradition requires a bell, book and candle. Words and their unfolding definitions serve here as the bell, tolling irregularly throughout. As for the book, well. What many of you call the Old Testament, I do not; it's not old if you don't accept the new. For me, there is the Torah, which is a scroll, not a book, and which was Greekified as the Pentateuch: the five (penta) books of Moses. Teuchos is an unusual word for book: referring to a case that held a papyrus scroll it means any kind of crafted container like a cup or bowl, because teuchein, like poiein, means to make. Even the word of God is part of the human enterprise of making, including the human enterprise of translation, which celebrates the plurality of languages and the possibility of communicating between them.

Many readers will know the five books as Genesis, Exodus, Leviticus, Numbers and Deuteronomy, a weird concatenation of Greek, Latin and English words. In the original Hebrew, the books do not have titles, but are known by their first words: Bereishit (In the beginning), Shemot (Names), Vayikra (And [He] called), Bamidbar (In the desert) and Devarim (Words/Things). I named the numbered chapters of this book after them: Beginning, Naming, Calling, Crying, No/Thing. After them, or in relation to them – the kind of relation who comes after, the bad child who questions everything.

I earned the right to use these titles by reciting them, in return for a felt pen, a phrase that profoundly describes how writing materialises my emotions. Brightly coloured, handheld, lambent with possibility: writing instruments have been a candle I've long carried before me to guide my way. I wanted that felt pen: it was the good kind, with the slimline tip and long-lasting ink reserve. If you could learn the names of all the fifty-four parshiot (chapters) of the Torah, you won the entire pack. So, I turned my memory, which was considered prodigious, to the list of Biblical Hebrew words. Not to their meanings, just to their sequence. I became the youngest-ever student to achieve victory, and it taught me that what you win is nausea. Because for all I could recite the titles of the parshiot, I could not recite their texts to the congregation in the weekly Sabbath synagogue service, unlike my father, who was acclaimed as a cantor. I was being taught religious studies, I was told in class, not for myself, but so I could educate my sons.

That's because I was assigned female at birth, and concomitantly defined and delimited by reproductive function. I no more accept this as a definition of femininity than I accept femininity as a definition of myself. I am non-binary, and I was assigned female: both have shaped my experiences since childhood, and shape the stories I tell here – both how and why I tell them, and struggle to tell them. Philological violence, like all violence, is directed at the vulnerable; in EW culture, that includes those of marginalised genders. Such a grouping is hard to articulate in the binary of English grammar and vocabulary, even more so when wrestling with legal definitions of sexual violence that are equally and exclusionarily binary. As speculative thinker and healer adrienne maree brown writes in her novel *Ancestors*, '*there's one true binary in this world. you are either mending or breaking the future.*' Mending the future means attending to past complexities and possibilities; in its past, the English word girl originally meant a child of any gender, and that is my past too.

I've forgotten more than the names of the parshiot: mending the future by attending to my past also, for me, means listening for ways to re-hear what I've forgotten, through trans, queer and feminist Jewish scholars and activists. I am grateful that they have given me safe words for entering into scenes with the tender and tendentious materials of my conservative religious upbringing, especially as I necessarily confront its entanglement with genocidal pious Zionism. 'No way round but through' is a phrase I overuse because it is painfully true.

I write this with a felt pen made up of the many ways that writers make themselves up. But there are only two writers whom I have been reading continuously since I learned to read: God, and Ursula K. Le Guin. Only one of them practised changing her mind, and thus changing mine. In each chapter, I offer one small example from her vast body of work, choosing moments when she revisited her best-known books and characters from a different point of view. Words and texts, like people, can change, and that is what makes them matter. Le Guin's (re)work(ing) gives me the sense of writing and speaking as being what Gertrude Stein called a 'continuous present', an ongoingness despite the fixity of print. Present participles, -ing words, were Stein's favourite part of speech. In English, they also act as gerunds, verbal nouns, as in 'the art of writing'. There's a lot to love about a word that just keeps going, and that can be two things at once.

My chapter titles were also inspired by Marina Warner's gerunding subtitle for *No Go the Bogeyman: Scaring, Lulling and Making Mock*. Warner's book profoundly influenced my understanding of how adults communicate with children, including the children in ourselves. In response, this book works through five functions of bad language that I have experienced since infancy, mapped on to the five books of Moses: Beginning/lying, Naming/consuming, Calling/

evacuating, Crying/blaspheming, and No/Thing/reifying. These are the ways that dominance shuts us down: the ways it de-faces and ef-faces us to render us all sur-face. To face up to it, we have to find a way to make up our faces that is not nostalgia for an inner child or outer Eden. To make up with each other is to enter into a new beginning by recognising that it was always there, in the deep past and in our memories.

The opposite of bad language is not good language, but rad(ical) languaging. Let's go, together, back to the roots.

1: BEGINNING

— to cut open, open up, gape open

I come from a family of liars. Families, plural, on either side. I come – another way of saying it – from families of immigrants. Of refugees fleeing persecution and telling the stories they needed to survive. A tangle of changed names, disavowed places, false documents, hazy memories, strategic omissions, misplaced papers, occluded languages, necessary narcissistic defences, and wilful self-deceptions. As in all family stories, there are touchstones for the polishing; charged, they touch my tongue to the live wires of history. Cossacks attacking, Nazis rising, stolen cutlery smuggled over borders in a coat hem; then, charabanc trips and Cable Street fights and gambling on the nags. These stories are not lies, but they lie. They offer cover for what's being untold – not just what is untold, but what is actively being removed from telling. What matters is what's not being articulated, because it cannot be. Lies are a bad beginning: a warning not to believe, that no one can be believed.

Arabic folk tales begin kan ya ma kan: it was and it was not. It's a phrase that teaches listeners to attend to a complex folding and unfolding of what might be real, what might be fantastical, and everything that shimmers in between. In English, we use the words story and tale to mean lies but also pleasurable fictional narrations. Sometimes we call a narration – but not a lie – an account, and in true English fashion we can hear it turn into accounting, and counting generally; one root of writing as mark-making is the tally stick of goods, and tally, tale and tell are all related. We can turn our other ear and hear accountability, a more recent formation dating to the Enlightenment, and cited as a quality of governance in the writing of John Stuart Mill among others. It has come to refer primarily to an ethical quality of individuals only in the last few decades, perhaps as governments have increasingly fore-gone any concept of it. To be accountable for one's accounts is to tell tales with an awareness of the toll of their telling.

Story comes from the classical Greek word historia, defined as knowledge obtained by inquiry. Historia comes from an older Greek word that dates back to the Homeric hymns: histor or istor, which means a judge, arbitrator, witness or expert, one who has the authority to certify a true account. Suddenly we are in the public courts, where a story can mean life or death. That history hangs over all our telling.

It does not have to. Istor comes to mean a judge because it means a knower. It comes from oida, the classical Greek verb that means to know, which has an unrelated-looking plural imperative – 'Iston!', meaning 'Let them know!' This root for historia suggests an older form of bearing witness, not to the court but to the community. 'Stories', writes literary scholar and activist for First Nations rights J. Edward Chamberlin, are

> ceremonies of belief as much as they are chronicles of events, even the stories that claim to be absolutely true. We first learn this when we are very young; which is to say, we learn how to believe before we learn what to believe ... and it is this practice that generates the power of stories.
>
> We need to go back to the beginning. We all want to believe.

He is writing in the context of colonial histories, or rather mis-stories, as the title of his book, *If This Is Your Land,*

Where Are Your Stories? Finding Common Ground, suggests. The title comes from a question asked by Haíɫzaqv (Heiltsuk) elders to white settlers in the place that the latter (mis)named British Columbia.

To set ceremony and belief first, before chronicle and event, is to upend the valorisation of facticity and objectivity, which underpin so many EW truth claims, despite their lack of roots. Setting ceremony and belief first reminds us to ask questions, because it holds us in the moment of telling before the start of the story itself: kan ya ma kan, once upon a time – or even, are you sitting comfortably? For Chamberlin, drawing on his experience of First Nations orature of the Pacific Northwest, story depends on its beginning – or rather, its beginning before the beginning. The deep breath, the coming-together, renegotiated as consent to believe each time, that allows words to work their spell.

The beginning before the beginning is present in one of the most famous of beginnings: in the King James Version of Genesis, there is a prepositional phrase, 'In the', to situate the beginning, or us within it. Bereishit, the first word in the Hebrew, does not exactly mean in the beginning – or rather it does, but it's complicated. It is a construct 'in direct grammatical dependence ... on the following verb,' writes liberation philologist Seth L. Sanders. 'Bereishit barah Elohim' is a single phrase, he says, meaning 'in the beginning *of* God's creating'. In the consonance of bereishit barah, b-r b-r, the first words echo each other: beginning and creating are impossibly intertwined. There is no such thing as a bare beginning, any more than any genesis is merely genetic. Bereishit is the beginning of something new, a change, which implies that there is a beginning before the beginning. Sanders points to one of the few other places where the word bereishit appears,

21

in Mishlei (Proverbs) 8, which is written in first person in the voice of Shekhinah, or Lady Wisdom. This abstract figure is associated with Asherata, an ancient Near Eastern female deity supposedly cast down by the Hebrew God. But before that, she was cast as his consort; and before that, she ruled alone.

This is not the ceremony of belief that I was given, although I was given the tools of literacy that allow me now, as an adult, to read it, recognise it, and grieve that it was not what I knew once upon a time. I was taught that bereishit meant in the beginning and that that beginning was God. Liberation philology is a powerful idea, a useful 'are you sitting uncomfortably?' that invites me to reflect on what I think I know. On the same day he posted 'An Early Rabbinic View of the First Word of Gensesis' to his blog Liberation Theology, Sanders also posted 'How do we tell the History of Israel after the Palestinian Genocide?', in which he poses a profound question:

> We who study the early history of the southern Levant
> often insist on placing it in a long arc culminating in
> the modern state of Israel. But what do we do when the
> arc of that history ends in a pile of rotting corpses?

This is not how I was taught to think about the history I was given. As Sanders demonstrates, we can rethink what we have learned by using the tools that we were given by the same schools and society that withheld information. I wield them not against the grain, but running along it, over and over, until the lies peel away from the core. Every tool is a weapon if you hold it right.

Words are weapons because they are rooted in weapons, especially the words that root us: umbilicus comes from the Latin word umbo, meaning the boss of a shield; vagina means sword sheath in Latin, before its anatomical usage; the Old English word for a human male was wapman, or weapon-man. Weapon, the *OED* notes compactly and euphemistically '(= membrum virile)'. There is no etymological link between weapon and penis, just an ideological one.

The words in which we begin are militant lies – but in their telling is something telling. They tell, as a liar is said to do, on themselves. As well as referring to the navel, umbo is the medical term for the central, most inverted portion of the ear drum, the cone-shaped membrane that transmits sounds from the air to the ossicles of the middle ear. It's the bit of your ear that, if you're hearing, makes you hear; the birth of sound. It's called after something defensive because it's vulnerable: it's where all the interior mechanisms of hearing in the middle ear and the brain connect to the onslaught of the world outside, umbilically. Imagine that instead of umbo, we used ambi-, the preposition that means both sides, now: here is where we meet, naming the navel and inner ear as going both ways, opening us to the world and the world to us. To get to the beginning before the beginning, I have learned that, wherever I am most shielded, that's where I have to be open. This is what begin means, when you look into its etymology: to cut or gape open, both the action of opening and the resultant being open. The mouth and the ear, those openings for speech and hearing, are both beginnings.

To be given into multiple languages is to sharpen your hearing. I am not fully bi+lingual, a word I'm coining as a companion to Helen Bowell's bi+sexual; perhaps I can call myself ambilingual, surrounded by and surrounding languages. I value the polyphonic complexity, but am left with a multiplied silence, the unspeakable gaps of half-truths hidden in the shifty slips between tongues. I was raised to listen to what I was being told, and ignore what was being unsaid, in three languages: English, Hebrew and Yiddish. I was taught prayers and songs in Aramaic and Ladino, although I was not taught to speak them; they were treated as if preserved in amber although both are in vivid living use today. Mostly, I was raised to assimilate into English, that Borg of a language that takes up what it finds useful from the people and cultures it attempts to discard or eviscerate. I spent many frustrating lessons on Hebrews, Biblical and modern, which I've mostly forgotten, or suppressed. Learning Biblical Hebrew did prepare me for studying Latin and classical Greek, languages learned on the page and in the dictionary, under the silencing weight of the canon.

My family didn't speak Yiddish, but rather smattered it macaronically into conversation. Yiddish is itself a fusion of German, Polish and Hebrew. It is written in Hebrew script, and printed in a semi-cursive font called vaybertaytsh, an early name for Yiddish itself, meaning women's language. It was expected that men could speak and read in Hebrew, and that women could not. This is one reason that Yiddish was rejected as a national language for the nascent State of Israel. From one side of my family, I heard a little Romanian and Romanian-inflected French; but of German, Russian or Lithuanian, the languages that would have actually been spoken day to day by my other great-grandparents – nisht. The languages that had cancelled their families, they cancelled. They were beyond the pale.

German was in fact warded off in my house with the sign of the evil eye, so I did not take the opportunity to learn it at school. But when I was struggling to the finish line of my thesis, I dreamed that I had found a book in the library by Virginia Woolf: *her* doctoral dissertation, written in German, on philological questions in Greek tragedy, German being the language of philology in the early twentieth century, and philological questions in Greek tragedy bearing no relation to my thesis whatsoever. Yet the book, in its existence and its detail, resolved all the problems I was having with my thesis and beyond. In the haze of climate-change, 33°C before 8am, I spent fifteen minutes naked at my desk, searching for this book on the university library catalogue, before realising that it had been a dream, one that gave Woolf the degree in Classics she had so wanted, as well as apparently giving me both the secrets of the universe and the (more astounding, to me at least) ability to read fluently in technical German.

This book is not that dream book. However much I liberate words or revive my ceremony of belief, I cannot go back and learn German in my teens when it was verboten to me, any more than history can revert to a situation where one side of my family would still be speaking German in Germany, or where Woolf would have been able to obtain a doctorate in Classics. But the speculative fiction of that dream is deep in this book: in the belief that an oneiric queer feminist liberation philology could, in fact, offer the secrets of the universe. That it could offer a way of listending through what Adrienne Rich succinctly called the 'lies, secrets and silence' that occur in individual families such as mine, because they are structured into cisheteropatriarchal colonial capitalism. Rich would deliberately omit the cis bit there, and it hurts my feminist heart that, given her creative, courageous and rigorous stands against oppression, she could not find it in the largesse of *her* heart to recognise trans women as women. A common language is only a dream if it includes all of us.

I have come back to the ceremony of belief that is palpable in my dream book: a yearning for language to be the key. I want to liberate philology because I want philology to liberate me, and words, and all of us. The dream book is a reminder that liberation can only happen in forms that exceed what is seen as strict rationality and linear chronicling. Dreams, jokes, analogies, gossip, tangents, folk tales and songs, dramatisations and speculations are considered bad language: tall tales that you are told off for telling. They are analogical, speculative and polyvalent modes that take time to understand. They require more than the brief instance of Samuel Taylor Coleridge's 'suspension of disbelief', with its suggestion of grinding stage machinery lifting a heavy, permanent and socially mandated curtain of scepticism. They require the listener and teller to begin before the beginning with negotiation of consent to believe. We have been forced to move fast, and so our ceremony of belief is broken.

Once upon a time there was time: time to listend to each other, to gather meaning together. Anthropologists call this 'high context', referring to a culture that is listening-intensive with an emphasis on sharing and testing knowledge collectively. Making time in which to make up listening relations is extremely inefficient, and efficiency is the watchword of colonial capitalism. Perhaps that's why the *Economist* called Tucuya 'the world's hardest language', a ridiculous claim as all languages are fluent for their communities. Spoken at the watershed of the Papuri, Inambú and Tiquié rivers in Amazonas, Tucuya has five evidentiality paradigms, according to linguist Janet Barnes; these are expressed as suffixes for verbs that indicate whether the source for your information is visual, obtained by other senses, apparent, second-hand, or assumed. In Tucuya, as in all languages, you can

26

lie, but – unlike in English – you cannot lie by omission or obfuscation. You have to provide a context for how you know what you're saying. Indo-European languages have two noun classes, referred to as genders, although words cannot have a gender, but Tucuya has somewhere between fifty and 140 classes specific to observations of the natural world of the watershed. It may be hard for outsiders to learn not because there are so many classes and suffixes, but because there is so much to observe, remember and respect. That takes time, such that 'once upon a time' becomes the mood all the time.

Recent EW studies show that storytelling for children who are patients in hospital can relax their muscles, as it decreases levels of cortisol, and releases oxytocin, a hormone that is synthesised in the brain in situations of trust, often reciprocally. Are you sitting comfortably? is a generous question, especially in a situation of pain, illness and constraint such as in a hospital. It implies that the speaker is also a listener: asking for your response, listending to you as an active participant in the ceremony, and then taking action to increase or ensure your comfort. In *If This Is Your Land...*, Chamberlin discusses how such storytelling between parents/carers and children is life-giving: it passes on cultural heritage and ethical guidance, undergirded by the biochemical mechanisms and bodily effects of taking time together engender a grounding sense of trust. It creates a vulnerability in which we are open.

When I was little, after Sabbath dinner on a Friday night, my siblings and I would go up to our shared bedroom in the half-light, and we would act out Grimms' fairy tales as my father half-read, half-told them. He gave us the Edwardian English bowdlerised picture-book versions in which all the fairies are little white girls in translucent dresses and the Ugly

Sisters do not cut off parts of their feet to fit into Cinderella's slippers. We were brave little tailors confronting dogs with eyes the size of dinner plates, and we were barefoot princesses tired with escaping the confines of princess life to go dancing. Brave and bold, these characters gave us routes out, ways to be and warnings to heed. 'Once upon a time', every time with the familiarity of prayer, spoken in a sing-song in the almost-dark where story, memory and dream might melt into one another in a tired child body, cued to trust by repetition of the ceremony and of patterns within the narratives. They all lived happily ever after. And when he was done telling the story, when it was dark, when no lights could be turned on because it was the Sabbath, my father would place his hand over my mouth and rape me.

The ceremony of belief can be used to lull, and while we want that to be the trust of a lullaby, the word is often followed by the phrase 'into a false sense of security'. The opposite of that kind of lull is will, as Sara Ahmed shows in *Living a Feminist Life*, in her reading of the disturbing tale collected by the Grimms as 'The Willful Child'. Yet as 'Little Red Riding Hood' warns us, stories can groom you so that you believe that you follow willingly, that what follows is what you will. It is not. I have been lulled falsely, and that makes the lull of belief difficult. When I tell this story about my childhood, it begins in a dreamspace that – because of its association with story, with speculation – seems to annul historia, my ability to witness.

It is not incidental that I was raped by the person who taught me to read and write, corrected my grammar, and stood for the authority of all the languages around me – legal, religious, familial-historical. Rape is the opposite of language: the opposite of meaning, of communication.

28

There is no listening. Rape is an erasure of shared existence, of the trust of being open. To be cut open is to begin.

To rephrase the KJV: in the beginning was the wound. But if there is a wound, then before the beginning there must have been something whole. There is no safe word, but there is the possibility, if just for a breath, of sanctuary. The English word asylum comes from the ancient Greek asylon, meaning both sanctuary – the protection of persons and things – and sacred virginity, because of its central meaning of inviolability. Sylē is a classical Athenian legal term meaning right of seizure, so a-sylē means without right of seizure. As a negative, a-sylum contains its opposite, and thus it is always a reminder that we are all vulnerable, asymmetrically so, to being assigned to the category of seizable, violable. That is where we have to begin.

In English, we cannot rebegin but we can restart, partially because start has within it both a sense of stopping and beginning again. Start is a merging of two distinct but broadly synonymous Germanic words. The first means to fall or cause to fall, as in 'you gave me a start!'; the second means to tighten or make rigid, and so be liable to fall. The word shifts, unpredictably, from meaning to make a sudden movement towards a more general kind of beginning. It is a curious theory of beginning as always starting over from a sudden start, from being startled. The suffix -le is a frequentative, so startling is starting over and over. Startle tells us that starting is a bodily flinch, a sudden tensing and sharp movement that is the opposite of relaxation into the ceremony of belief. The startle reflex starts behind our umbo, in the deep place that it protects. Noises over eighty decibels alert the cochlea to send neural signals through the back of the neck to the limbs, in order to move the body away from the negative stimulus.

My childhood was full of spank and spake. That's what God is: a rod and a hard word, a loud commandment to be seen, not heard, to listen and obey. This commandment had the effect of making listening a punishment because of shame at being open. I thought I was offering a reception, but I was ordered to be a receptacle. Listening is associated with other activities that ask you to be an orifice, to be receptive and penetrable – most obviously, as that linguistic cluster suggests, with sexual activity. Listening, like other forms of receptiveness and penetrability, is then cast as passive, as submissive. Cisheteropatriarchal EW Christian culture cannot imagine that bottoming can be consensual or pleasurable, and goes out of its way to eradicate the possibility through fixed hierarchies – fixed in the sense that switching is not admitted, and that topping and bottoming (which is also mapped onto other hierarchies) have fixed values of superiority and inferiority. To embrace bottoming, or listening, is a form of resistance, but dominance condemns it as the foregoing of personhood. It's deep in EW culture that the only way to be a full, real, recognised person is to be active, penetrative, dominant, commanding. Listening is placed on the other side of the Aristotelian binary, in the hole of non-personhood.

Being spoken to, being language-spanked until you obey, means giving up your right to reply – that is, your right to independent and critical thought. Your fight-or-flight response kicks in, which can freeze speech. This is where a restart(le) can be so generative, a regeneration out of stuckness, such that we can rethink listening as a space of possibility rather than punishment. In *Living a Feminist Life*, Ahmed refers to this as 'feminist snap', a sharp noise that prompts us to realise we are frozen and to find the tools and allies to get free. In *Doppelganger*, Naomi Klein describes how John Berger surprised her by writing that one of her earlier books, *The Shock Doctrine*,

> 'provokes and instils a calm'. When people and societies enter into a state of shock, they lose their identities and their footing, he observed. 'Hence, a calm is a form of resistance' ..., the condition under which we return to ourselves.

A start(le) or shock offers an opportunity to take heed and reset after a bad beginning – and having admitted we have made a bad beginning, to admit that we need to make ourselves up and make up with ourselves.

Think of the Fool in the Tarot, the zero card, the card before the first card. They are often depicted stepping confidently, like Wile E. Coyote, off a cliff. The Fool's fall iconicises the start(le) that Sigmund Freud calls parapraxis: the trip that, whether physical or verbal (which is after all physical, on the tip of your tongue), starts up from the unconscious to startle you into listening to yourself. It is also, Freud claims, a reminder that you have to listen to yourself at the level of the parapraxis, which happens beneath the ordered flow of verbal language and formal gestures that supposedly demonstrate your adult control of your body. 'Nein,' says Siggi. It's not what you consciously say that matters; it's what you unconsciously say: accidentally, gesturally, disastrously.

Are you sitting uncomfortably, on the ground, having stepped confidently only to stumble and fall? To fall physically, phonically, semantically, is an embarrassment. We would rather force ourselves up again than admit to being down. We would rather lie to ourselves that we are strong and stable. Lying down, like listening, is cast as passive; to be told that one is taking something lying down suggests that we are being punished or inviting punishment.

To lie down and to lie rather than tell the truth are homophones with no etymological relationship. This happens: words, like all of us, don't have to be related on a family tree to become close to one other. Lie and lie are not quite antonymic homophones or homographs, such as cleave, which has two diametrically opposed meanings – to join, and to separate – that have converged on the same spelling and pronunciation from different roots. Lie and lie have instead converged in moral value, if not semantic content; there is a sense in EW culture that both lying down and telling a lie are infantile, uncivilised, spineless, opposed to the morally upright.

Jacob Grimm was collecting (or stealing) folk tales to forge a Volk consciousness for the newly unified Germany; of course, this nationalist project also required a comprehensive German dictionary, which he compiled. In the process, he looked into the etymology of the German word for lie. *OED* etymologist Anatoly Liberman notes that 'the words for lying exist in all the Indo-European languages, and not a single one of them has a clear origin' – but Grimm had a go. He decided that there must be a link between two fourth-century Gothic homophones: liugan, meaning to tell a lie, and liugan, a legal term meaning to marry a man. In order to connect the words, he made an intuitive and evidence-free leap that liugan (in the sense of to marry a man) must have originally meant to conceal or veil; 'whether', says Liberman, one is concealing 'facts or the bride'. Within this witty comment, as in Grimm's linguistic prestidigitation, is the implication that all heterosexual marriages are lies told by women, because all brides are bed tricks like Leah and Rachel in Bereishit.

Marital rape was, for a long time, a lie, because it was legal (and therefore not rape) in the UK until the landmark court judgment in *Regina respondent and R appellant* in 1991. The judgment was only codified into law a decade later, in the controversial Sexual Offences Act 2003, which, among other things, attempted, awkwardly, to provide a legal definition of consent. According to the United Nations Population Fund's report 'My Body Is My Own', in 2021 there were forty-three countries, many of them coerced into British colonial legal structures, that still had no legislation criminalising marital rape. The Law of the Father, the Husband and the Unholy Empire persists. What we can learn from that is that the marriage contract is a lie, not because it is a trick, but because it is fixed. Only one partner has the legal right to enter into contract, so by the very act of marrying under traditional laws, a woman is made to lie. Under patriarchy, she is only permitted to give consent to giving up her consent.

In dominance culture, everyone non-dominant is assigned lying at birth. Perpetrators deny, attack, and reverse victim and offender (known as DARVO) because they can, because victims have no standing. We can't argue back, because we are, by our very embodiments, liars. You cannot state that you have been raped, because anyone who is vulnerable to rape is a liar, because they are a lying-down-type, one who is submissive and vulnerable, assuming a position associated with infants. You cannot lie down and speak out. In-fans literally means non-speaking. Baby gives us the frequentative babble; they both derive from 'ba', a supposedly nonsense syllable, as seen in the word barbarian, meaning someone who says ba-ba.

So, to speak from an embodiment associated by dominance with lying down is to be a liar, because you constitutionally cannot speak. The more you protest you are not lying, the more it is used as evidence that you are.

To startle ourselves into speaking against power, the first thing we must say is that power lies: to us, about us, to erase us. Listen to Caroline Darian as she repeats the word lie and its variants four times in two sentences in a courtroom in Avignon in 2024. 'You are a liar. I am sick of your lies, you are alone in your lie, you will die lying.' She was speaking on the stand after evidence came to light that made her a co-plaintiff in a trial that took place in public at the insistence of plaintiff Gisèle Pelicot, Caroline's mother, after years of rape by her husband and dozens of other men. The accused admitted raping his wife, and arranging for other men to rape her after he had drugged her, but denied raping his daughter. 'He denied it,' Darian told Agence France-Presse, 'but he also lied several times and gave different versions of the story during the two and a half years of the investigation.' A lying liar lies.

The French for to lie, mentir, has had a very different etymological journey. Mentir originates from the Latin word for mind, mens. The Latin verb mentior initially means to think quickly or be inventive, but it shifts from a positive to a negative, to telling a tall tale. Its older meaning is still audible, however, such that Darian's repetition also resonates as something like: 'I am sick of this brain-in-a-jar shit, you are rendered solipsistic by being caught in the assumption of your mental superiority, and insisting on it means you will die alone.'

Mind over body is the paradigmatic Aristotelian duality, with all the lying-down-types lined up with embodiment.

The question of who is believed depends on the idea of intelligence. Language use is still seen as the quality that defines human intelligence as different from, and superior to, that of other beings, and there is still an equally pervasive and pernicious related hierarchy that classifies humans as more or less intelligent according to perceptions of their intelligibility, or language use. Both intelligence and intelligibility are rooted in eugenicist lies.

Intelligence derives from the Latin verb inter+legere, meaning to gather between. Inter means between, amid, among, as well as during or while; that is, inter in its broadest sense refers to whatever is within, whether spatially or temporally. It is the inside of ambi-'s outside. Legere, the root of the word Logos, the Word, from which English gets the word logic, is usually cited as meaning to read. Intellegere might therefore appear to mean 'to read between [the lines]', which is how it is used in the sense of intelligencing, or spying. But legibility does not begin with words on the page; it draws on older skills of gathering information from the world. Deep in the roots of legere are older forms associated with gathering and tending to crops, not words.

It's no big surprise that the word for word goes back to the living world, and to practices related to growing and making both food and textiles. In her compendious book *Fabric: The Hidden History of the Material World*, Victoria Finlay starts by noticing how many common English words for words go back to textile-making, starting with the word text itself. My favourite is that a clew (clue) is originally a ball of yarn, such as Ariadne used to solve the labyrinth. It makes sense that making food and fabrics together, which would have taken up most of people's time, would be the site of mutual (s)aid.

It stands to reason that the words we use for wording would be rooted in those everyday, embodied activities of world-making – but it has been obscured, as Ursula K. Le Guin writes in her essay 'The Carrier Bag Theory of Fiction', because 'it is hard to tell a really gripping tale of how I wrested a wild-oat seed from its husk, and then another, and then another ... No, it does not compare, it cannot compete with how I thrust my spear deep into the titanic hairy flank.' We have to listend for the word in the wild oat and the wild oat in the word. They arise in tending: in a practical, mutual sociability that is high context, where evidentiary paradigms might be tested over slow, communal tasks, such that truth is intelligible: gathered bodily between us.

There is a synonym for telling and accounting that is available for this act, which suggests collective practice, and it is relating. In the context of Genesis and other bad families, relation as a synonym for storytelling brings a whole host of complications, but it also offers a reminder that kinship is a set of stories as well as a place where stories are told and tested. Relating begins with the Latinate prefix re-, again, as in repeat, relive, refuse, reveal. The story loops around, another start(le) that shocks us into beginning again the long process of hearing ourselves as speaking subjects who deserve a listending that leads to action.

This is what Chilean poet and artist Cecilia Vicuña is unravelling in her collection *Palabrarmas*, a title that could translate as s/wordwork. Palabra means word, armas means weapons and labrar means to work – particularly physical work such as farming, carving and embroidery. Palabra comes from parabola, which in its original Greek has meanings to do with both story and mathematics. Its basic sense indicates two things placed alongside each other, which can refer to an astronomical or geometric conjunction or to a parable, a story that has two or more levels of meaning. In *Palabrarmas*, Vicuña moves through parabolas:

> But throughout history words have concealed and revealed, constantly transforming.
>
> Having lost the memory of the original meaning, we can invent an etymon (true meaning), one that contains within what the word will be. To go backward and inward simultaneously. To contemplate the origins and the future. The ancient and current signified.

> REVELAR   to reveal
> VOLVER A VELAR   to re-veil

Heard here in Suzanne Jill Levine and Eliot Weinberger's translation, Vicuña re-covers in order to recover. She remembers the role of the veil, which brides traditionally wore to mark their inviolability, a-sylum, which precedes and supersedes the claims of the law and patriarchy. She (re)turns the veil into an ethical imperative to make words up reparatively from a marginalised, dissident perspective, to turn against the made-up things of dominance culture.

Although I was trained in the practice of Mishnah – textual wrangling, rabbinical-style – at my faith primary school, and was taught how to hunt an etymology through my classical education, it is poets such Vicuña whom I honour in seeking meaning in liberation philology. Vicuña is a guide to words and unwording: her act of revelation is an act of return, one that is nonlinear such that we can work from 'what the word will be'. It's not just that the ending of the story is always present in the beginning, but that the end can re-turn and alter the beginning with a start. Vicuña startles us into listening again, to what is before the beginning.

I say this now because I didn't say it then, and I have to believe in the possibility of the start(le), of volver, of accounting for relation. Of re-covering.

What if your toddling body keeps speaking what words cannot? Here are some of the ways my child body articulated, desperate to find any language that could be heard and believed: vomiting after meals; 'growing pains' so bad I couldn't walk upstairs; sleep paralysis; deep bruising and frequent eczema on my inner thighs; repeated broken bones; second-degree burns; extremely early puberty; high fevers every school holiday. An 'involuntary' suicide attempt when I was twelve, described as a swimming accident, left me with visibly damaged front teeth and an embodied, enraged sense of why the most recent Conservative government designedly underfunded dentistry for a decade, because orthodontic and buccal pain and shame can both, and synergistically, cause you to fall silent.

No one heard a thing. No one was listening. No one knew how to listen.

I can ask myself why I didn't speak out about the abuse then, or I can listen to my self now, and to how I was not heard. How I learned to listen to the pluripotent polyvalences of non-verbal speech, to lie down and acknowledge the lies I was telling myself, is another story. Bound up in it is a dream that turned out – unlike Woolf's PhD – to be not a dream, but a book.

For over two decades, I dreamed repeatedly of being trapped on winding paths in an underground cavern, in a ritual I couldn't determine, moving through set patterns of steps, haunted or hunted, waking terrified that I was going to die. A year after the memories of the abuse returned in the middle of my PhD, I was assigned to teach Le Guin's *Earthsea* series. As I re-read *A Wizard of Earthsea*, I felt again the annoyance I'd felt when the book had been read to us by our Year 3 teacher: that it was all about boys. I thought that the annoyance had stopped me there, and that I hadn't read any further Le Guin until I was a queer teenager rapt by *The Left Hand of Darkness*. When I turned to the second book in the *Earthsea* series, *The Tombs of Atuan*, I realised with a falling startle that I was re-reading it, tripping over another buried memory. It was Le Guin who had described the labyrinth I had been fleeing through. In the book, it runs beneath the sacred tombs, a vast snarl of dark passages that only the priestess of the tombs is allowed to navigate by a map held only in memory.

My unconscious had stayed true to Le Guin's parable about the dangers of orthodox faith, but lied protectively in casting it as a dream. Living and learning in a queer feminist community in my twenties, I was for the first time able to listend to myself, and to the harrowing and healing collectively held. Until that moment, I had not been intelligent: I had not been gathered, nor been attentive to what could be gathered within a consensual community.

And so I re-read: Tenar, the priestess, finds a trespasser in the labyrinth. She is mandated to kill him, but she listends to him – because he listends to her. It is not easy or painless, much like the listending I was doing in my own life. The walls of Atuan fall, and it is terrible. Everything Tenar knows about her world collapses. She realises, painfully, that she has bought into the illusion of power proffered in exchange for her confinement. What I had to admit to myself was the fact of the abuse, yes. And more than that: that the power promised to me through obeisance to both conservative Jewishness and Englishness was a lie. Silenced by dominance, I had stayed silent because of that promise: that at some point my story would make sense, that its beginning would be justified through its ending, because I would become the one with the power to speak.

That is not what happens to Tenar. She does not become a wizard. She does not learn a magic phrase, or confront and defeat the cruel people who have imprisoned her with an impassioned speech. She does not return to her prior life. *The Tombs of Atuan* is a book of silences, and a crash: a shock that leads to calm, a feminist snap. Towards the end of the book, Tenar, still in the start(le) of that crash, begins again. As is one of her great strengths, Le Guin does not make beginning easy, but offers it as a painful vulnerability: a s/wordwork that cuts open the face of a lie; a salt and wet wound worn on the face as a marker of having to start again. Tenar cries out, and it is the beginning of a new story:

> A dark hand had let go its lifelong hold upon her heart.
> But she did not feel joy, as she had in the mountains.
> She put her head down in her arms and cried, and her
> cheeks were salt and wet. She cried for the waste of
> her years in bondage to a useless evil. She wept in pain,
> because she was free.

2: NAMING

— nomen est omen (the name is a sign/fate)

Are you sitting uncomfortably? Let's begin again.

> ther was a pensull
> a bunny et th pensull
> it was a shap shap pensull
>   end.

Eat lead, reader! I quote, with permission (and commission), my middle nibling's first, last and masterpiece work. The pensull, which is doing the writing, is definitely the protagonist, not the bunny. By the end of the story, the instrument of its creation has been eaten, and has killed its devourer. This is brilliant revenge on the unnerving act of writing, and on the reader's hungry eyes on the page. In *No Go the Bogeyman*, Marina Warner quotes Adam Phillips to the effect that 'kissing could be described as aim-inhibited eating'. The same is true of reading or listening, as, xwélmexw scholar and artist Dylan Robinson (Stó:lō/Skwah) theorises in his term 'hungry listening', for the ways in which white settler colonial listeners consume Indigenous music.

Warner is writing about how the wish-fear of 'eating and being eaten inspires one of the most common games adults play with babies ... going "Grrrrrrr, you're good enough to eat."' In *Impersonal Passion: Language as Affect*, Denise Riley writes that one affective power of language is to consume us. She links 'the small violence' of parents naming a child to God naming the stars, because 'the mute infant bearer is no better placed to object than they, though the godlike parental

41

tyranny of naming will play out its repercussions for the rest of that child's life'. Riley's work as a poet and scholar is known for its precision, its refusal to rely on language's lull. Her influential earlier book, *'Am I That Name?': Feminism and the Category of 'Women' in History* follows Simone de Beauvoir in recognising that womanhood is socially constructed. Furthermore, writes Riley, it is linguistically constructed: any useful and meaningful feminism has to recognise and indeed revel in the ambiguity and historical contingency of the term 'woman', rather than wielding it as a fixed and exclusionary identity. Riley's is feminism as liberation philology. She reminds us that while our relationship status to words may be set to 'it's complicated' due to their hot mess of context and usage, our commitment to solidarity and liberation for all can remain steadfast and unconditional. *Impersonal Passion* builds on the argument about 'woman' as a problematic name to suggest that this may be true of all names, specific and general, because of their fixity in a mutable world.

'Nomen est omen' is used as a proverb, a classical Latin tag meaning one's name is one's fate or destiny, or at the very least, if interpreted rationally, a sign of one's future profession. In 1994, *New Scientist* magazine coined the hypothesis of nominative determinism, the playful idea that there is a causal relationship between someone's given and/or family name and their career or actions. But the origins of this numinous idea are in fact ominous: 'Nomen est omen' is an abbreviation of a line from a play by Plautus, in which one slave is persuading his master to buy another as a sex worker, a woman called Lucris (as in lucre). He says what amounts to, 'With a name like that, she's worth it at any price'.

'Am I that name?' is a fair question here, in the playwright's misogynistic set-up. Lucris does not speak: her name speaks for her, and speaks only in tongues of money – not accruing to her, but to her owner. Yet the phrase passes into usage by shedding these exploitative specificities of class and gender, which are not inherent in a person but circumstantial and contextual. Names are omens because of their fixity, which is attributed to their essentialism: a name *names* some aspect of us that is then considered inescapable. Our potential for being otherwise, Riley suggests, is consumed by that name. Having been named, we then cannot speak against it because we cannot speak from outside it. 'A name can be changed later on by its bearer,' she adds, 'but it takes fervent toughness to insist on it'. It is hard to speak of yourself as not being yourself, to say that you are not that name that has come to define you, because then: who is speaking? To speak against your name is to be returned to being the 'mute infant bearer', the in-fans who cannot speak for themselves in ways that are audible or legible, because it is adults who adjudge value and meaning.

When the child Tenar is serving in the tombs of Atuan, her name is Arha, which means the Eaten One. She has been taken from her parents very young, as she is seen as a reincarnation of all the previous Arhas. She is inducted into this role through a terrifying ceremony where her given name, Tenar, is 'eaten' by the God she serves. This is an especially terrifying idea in Earthsea. In *A Wizard of Earthsea*, the first book in the series, the young wizard Ged goes to the magical island of Roke to learn, above all, the power of names – including their power to maim and kill. Tenar's un-naming is a profoundly injurious act, one that removes her from herself, like the carceral assignation of numbers in place of names. The forcible act of re-naming eradicates self-knowledge and ways of articulating it; we may cling to our previously assigned names out of familiarity, a defence of what is known – not because it is true or real, but because it pre-exists the new imposition.

What could be called naming-downwards, as opposed to self-naming or defending one's name, acts as a delimitation and a leash: you are what I say of you, and nothing else. Like most acts of dominance, naming-downwards rests on a vexed paradox: that those subjected to it are inherently empty or absorbent, so that the name or other violence will take hold; and that they are also inherently resistant, such that the name or other violence is necessary to subdue them. At base, these are both the same claim: that those subjected to dominance are not rational actors, in both their impression-ability and their intransigence, and so must be controlled and contained.

Censorship, like naming, arises from and within this paradox, targeting those it construes as both impressionable and resistant due to their non-rationality. Children and young people are the paradigmatic targets: censorship of materials relating to gender and sexuality is predicated on a claim to impressionability. I think about the chapter book I read most as a child, *The Diary of Anne Frank*. It was as centred in my primary education as it was censored – not that I knew it at the time. The diary's significance was staked on its claim to authenticity, which also seemed to promise completeness. Why would some of Anne's diary have been hidden away in a Secret Annex? It was only in 1986 that a revised critical edition was published, which included Anne's original diary, her own edited version, and the famous published version as edited by her father, Otto Frank. Among passages that Otto had removed, that edition revealed, were Anne's thoughts about girls and boys on whom she had had crushes at school, and about her own changing adolescent body, which she examined as intently and intimately as she did the relationships and details of her constrained life in the Annex. Forced into hiding, she hid nothing of herself from herself. General non-scholarly readers did not have access to the Anne who wrote about her clitoris until a new translation of the revised edition by Susan Massotty in 1995. For many younger readers, the restored passages wouldn't have been available until the graphic novel by Ari Folman and David Polonsky in 2016, which since publication has been one of the most challenged books in schools in the US, on the grounds of its references to sexuality and human anatomy.

Silence=Death, to uphold one of the best-known slogans of the AIDS crisis. The iconic poster, created in 1987 by a consciousness-raising group of the same name, used and inverted the pink triangle assigned to gay men in the Nazi death camps to draw parallels between the Holocaust and the deathly silence around HIV/AIDS. A sign is also a name, in its way: omen est nomen. The group later joined the AIDS activism group ACT UP, who deployed the poster widely. In 2024, ACT UP produced a badge and T-shirt with the pink triangle transformed into an equally iconic slice of watermelon, a sign of Palestinian resilience. The polyvalent new symbol highlights the parallels between the genocidal threats to the communities, and embraces the parallels between queer and Palestinian liberation as forms of bodily and nominative autonomy.

When I think about the protests I have been on, it is this confluence of autonomies that I feel in my body. I remember going on my first, at around the time I would have been reading *The Tombs of Atuan* and *The Diary of Anne Frank*. It was in my school friend's kitchen and living room, organised by her older sister and her sister's best friend, who persuaded us and a number of stuffed animals to participate. It was exhilarating: we banged pots and pans, while shaking our crayoned signs at the ceiling and yelling, 'WE PROTEST! STRIPTEES ARE THE BEST!' I didn't know what a strip-tee was, but I respected the rights of my friend's cool older sister and her friend to play their favourite game (throwing their T-shirts at each other and cackling, I later found out), which my friend's mother had outlawed. Strip teas! Striped ease! It sounded so good, so relaxing, so free, some meld of food and body and colouring and clothing and lying down and play. And the rhyme of protest and best? Chef's kiss. An iconic image or slogan can be a way of naming a silence, holding an urgent space open where a more complex semant-ics can take the time to be formed. But first the silence has to be named.

I could not name the sexual abuse I experienced because the sex education I had was limited by both state and synagogue. Many of my primary classmates went on to attend twinned gender-segregated faith schools; at the school designated for girls, the GCSE biology textbook section on the penis and testes was excised, in an incident that made tabloid news. Yet it was not news that my biology textbook, at my secular school, could not mention non-heterosexual sex and relationships because of Section 28. So much EW educational policy is focused on curtailing both bodily and nominative autonomy, so that we are educated out of a sense of our right to name ourselves and what is happening in and to our bodies, beginning with the basic right to say No, to name our refusal.

Since 2013, autonomy, speaking out, and refusal to con-form to authority have been pathologised as oppositional defiant disorder (ODD), a diagnosis that can lead to med-ication and even incarceration. In the US, where the term was coined, it is transparently used to target poor Black and Latino young men disproportionately, with the aim of placing them in for-profit youth detention. In the UK, the diagnosis appears to be used by the NHS primarily for young people with ADHD. A document published by Essex Partnership University NHS Foundation Trust names the behaviours on which diagnosis is based with non-clinical, judgemental terms such as 'stubborn, hostile ... angry or resentful, spiteful or vindictive'. These labels are applied to vulnerable young people as symptoms of a so-called disorder, even though the document itself acknowledges that ODD-identified behaviours often occur when there are environmental causes, such as abusive parenting or ableist school cultures. There are good reasons to refuse to comply, and that is why refusal is punished.

In 1980 and 1981, Irish political prisoners incarcerated by the British government went on hunger strike. I did not know, because I was a toddler, and it was not the sort of news that was covered on *Newsround*. But when I was seven, a few years after the deaths of Bobby Sands and nine others, I stopped eating. Controlling what goes in and out of one's mouth is one of the most broadly accessible forms of protest for those who are constrained, along with refusing to speak. There was only one edible foodstuff in my primary school lunches, steamed chocolate pudding, and that was ruined forever the day when a canteen worker topped it with gravy instead of the (identical-looking, to be fair) hot chocolate sauce. The food at my primary school was bland, institutional, monotonous and borderline inedible, it was true, and I articulated it as my reason for refusing to eat.

It was true – and it was a lie of omission, hiding the unspeakable reasons. My refusal to eat led the family doctor to name me 'a spoiled little madam'. I was spoiled, in the sense that the chocolate pudding was. The doctor, however, was referring to the same quality of wilfulness that is now pathologised as ODD. I did indeed have a desire to assert my will on the world: to see whether by not eating I could be not eaten. However wilful I was, I could not not be eaten, because my body did not belong to me. Under conservative Judaism, and indeed as a general EW principle, it belonged first to God, then to my father, then to my husband, handed, like Lucris, from one to the next without my say.

Except I kept trying to have a say. The year before I stopped eating, I stopped responding to the name on my birth certificate, and would only respond to the shortened version. Maybe this was prompted by Tenar, after absorbing or being absorbed by *The Tombs of Atuan* so deeply and completely that it reconfigured my unconscious. I had Biblical precedent: there are several examples in the Torah of name changes being holy, significant and respected, if also stressful. Abraham starts out as Avram, given a new name by God when he is circumcised at the age of ninety-nine. Jacob, so good they renamed him twice, is called Israel first by the angel he wrestles and defeats, and then again by God when he arrives in Bethel. So far, so father of the nation. I turned instead to Nevi'im, to the Book of Judges, to a figure I had played in a school play. Unlike the patriarchs who take up their God-given monikers, Naomi renames herself. After the death of her husband and sons, she chooses Mara, meaning bitter like the sea. Her name refers to her grief, but also to her non-status as a sonless widow in a patriarchal culture. She has so few ways to access food that she and her daughter-in-law Ruth become gleaners, those who gather the fallen grain behind the harvesters. Facing destitution,

Mara turns to her own name as a small but possible space in which she can resist. In an oral culture where a name is a kinship marker, however, she risks disappearing herself from all social structures of recognition.

Our names are, for the most part, no longer spoken accounts of ourselves and our relational responsibilities. Ceremonies of belief via declaration have been replaced by paperwork, such that changing your name now risks bureaucratic death, an exit from all records and resources. I have changed my name twice as an adult according to English law, and what I can tell you is that the process is designed to prevent you from changing your name because it greatly inconveniences the state when you do. The state does not want you to change your name, and works to associate it with criminality and degeneracy, with an underlying accusation that you are eluding both surveillance and patrilineality. Unless, of course, you are a cis woman getting married to a cis man and taking his name (transferring ownership to him). If you don't do this, and you have children, the questions of their last names and of parental recognition by the state become complex. If you do take his name, then the government, banks, phone companies, travel ticket issuers and so on will happily accommodate you without question.

Even though the data systems are presumably exactly the same, it is somehow not possible for them to do this if you change your name due to transition, divorce or other reasons, including, for example, to evade a stalker or persecution. Digital security has created an additional layer of intransigence, where we are attached to our names-as-usernames, which must match with the names on our documents, and to our email addresses as tokens of identification. It was harder to change my name with my mobile service provider than with the government.

It is the latter, however, who, in this digital era, still demands a cheque. Checks and balances are the securitised logic we accept as supposed protection in exchange for being locked ever tighter into the contract that is a fixed name. In a data-extractive, surveillant worldview, nomen ever more omen est.

A name is how not only a parent, but also the paternalist and patriarchal state, consumes you into subjecthood. Here is one of my paternal great-grandfathers at the British border, fleeing pogroms with documents in an illegible and therefore illegitimate language, Russian or Lithuanian, giving his name, one that remains unknown to me. Unable to read them, the state official randomly assigned my arriving refugee ancestor a stereotypical Jewish name, one that meant our completely unrelated next-door neighbours had the same last name, in order to be legible to the assimilationist state. Surnames are legal fictions as much as is fatherhood; sur from super-, meaning after, but given that surnames are often patronymics it feels like sir. They attach you at once to patrilineage and to state surveillance. We are betrayed by our need to be named, which leads us to bow to being eaten by the border and its ordering.

Louis Althusser coined the term interpellation for this form of consumption. As a Marxist theorist, he was looking for an explanation as to why people submit to what he called the ideological state apparatuses (ISAs), that contain and control us. He argued that people are neither stupid nor passive, so there must be some reward in answering the state's call. English translations of Althusser's work use as standard the neutral term hail for interpeller, but in Latin, interpellare is a startling term. It means to hinder or obstruct, to accost or disturb, and to harass or even hit on: it is an unwanted, disruptive speech act that implicitly mobilises a power differential. Althusser agrees that interpellation is an inter-ruption – but one that causes us to feel seen and included because the state is addressing us. It's a powerful idea: that accepting the state calling our names, even to violate us, gives us standing within it, a standing we can activate. This is borne out by Althusser wielding his understanding of the state, and the status afforded by his white, cishet male and class privilege, to avoid prison after murdering former resis-tance fighter and leading sociologist (and sexual abuse survi-vor) Hélène Rytmann, his wife, and to retain his name as a credible, oft-cited philosopher.

Once we have been named and accepted the fixity of that naming, it becomes ever more difficult to refuse the orders of the ISAs. This is the flaw in the now widely quoted and decon-textualised instruction from Timothy Snyder's handbook *On Tyranny*, in fact the book's first and central lesson: 'Do not obey in advance.' According to Snyder, 'Most of the power of authoritarianism is freely given. In times like these, individu-als think ahead about what a more repressive government will want, and then offer themselves without being asked. A citizen who adapts in this way is teaching power what it can do.' While Snyder's five-word slogan may feel like an empowering instruction to be one's better self, his fuller account of this obedience depends on the assumption that we are all, always and only, rational beings ('think ahead') and that the state does not already know what it can do and is doing with its power. It is a liberal fantasy of individual agency, and suggests that any government is not by nature repressive. If you have been named, if you have accepted your fixity in the social order, you have already obeyed, because it benefits you.

Althusser argues that we are impressionable: our names are hard to disobey because they make an impression on us, sinking (their teeth) into us. To be interpellated is to be the Eaten One who has something to eat; to not be interpellated is to risk starvation. Tenar, renaming herself by reclaiming her childhood name, and Mara, renaming herself to describe her new life, offer examples we can follow, signs pointing to a way out.

The book that Jews know as Shemot (meaning Names) is called Exodus, meaning a going out, from the Pentateuch to the King James Version and beyond. The relation is coincidental, a suggestive association that what the Jews are exiting is being named. They're not: having been named from on high by God, the Israelites enter into that interpellation, claiming privilege and status by colonising lands in the name of the Namer. Zionism, like cisheteropatriarchy, is naturalised by referencing the Torah, as Seth L. Sanders points out, but also by the British government as part and parcel of its imperialist history. Mixe linguistic activist Yásnaya Elena Aguilar Gil writes, in Ivonne Santoyo-Orozco's English translation, that 'Modern states fundamentally rely on the development of nationalist practices that create the illusion of a common past, a shared identity, and the need for a single language.' The linguistically bordered nation-state practices language as border and border guard – but it does so under an older religious imprimatur.

Shibboleth is a word that draws a border, and makes that border deadly: in the Book of Judges, it leads to 42,000 deaths. This story is often ignored or mistold when the word is used or misused: it has come to mean a secret that differentiates us from them, and its history is carried in that secretive way, too. Shibboleth in fact means something that carries something else within it: it is the part of a plant that contains the grain, such as the ears of corn or wheat that Ruth and Mara were gleaning.

It's an ancient root that once again roots language in gathering plants to make food and clothing. But it is stripped to a husk. What remains of shibboleth is that it begins with sh-, the Hebrew letter shin (as in Shin Bet, the Zionist security agency).

Back in the days of the Judges, the people on one side of the river Jordan, the Gileadites, led by the Israelite judge Jephthah (yes, the one who sacrificed his daughter) pronounced it sh-, but the people on the other side of the river, the Tribe of Ephraim (the territory that includes Bethel, where Jacob got named Israel, again), pronounced it s-. When the Gileadites beat back an incursion by the Ephraimites, they dammed the river and interrogated anyone crossing, commanding them to say shibboleth. Those who pronounced it sibboleth were killed. They were defeated troops returning to their own land by crossing back over the river Jordan. A single letter meant death to 42,000 people, close to the number of Palestinian deaths between that river and the sea as certified in the year after 8 October 2023 by the Health Ministry in Gaza (although the *Lancet* estimated that the real death toll, to that date, was most likely nearly double that figure). That's a staggering number of deaths, a devastating difference to be caused by a single letter. This is why shibboleth now means a speech act that can be life-or-death. There is no balm from Gilead: might equals right pronunciation.

The reason for this accented test is not the singularity but the multiplicity of s/sh/z sounds in Semitic languages. Semitic is itself a sibboleth, in multiple senses. Nineteenth-century EW philologists decided to name a group of related languages that includes Aramaic, Arabic and Hebrew as Semitic, from the name of Noah's son Shem. Classical Greek did not have a sh- sound, so Shem becomes Sem in the Pentateuch. So, S(h)emites are the people descended from

Shem. They are also the People of the Name, because Shem, as well as being a name, means name, as in the book Shemot. Jews who want to avoid saying the sacred Tetragrammaton, the four-letter name of God given in English as Yahweh, use the circumlocution HaShem, the Name. Just as Jacob was named Israel twice over, so too Semitic is overdetermined even as it loses its association with a name, the Name and naming. S(h)em was selected by philologists as the genus name for the language group not on the basis that he is the (eldest or second eldest) son of Noah, but because he is the direct ancestor, nine generations down, of Abraham. Nominativity is patriarchy, begetting and begetting.

Greek, whose alphabetic system derived from Phoenician, itself a Semitic language, kept a plurality of x and z sounds, but shed its sh-. Hebrew, on the other hand, has letters that are sounded Ts or Tz as well as two different Ss, a Sh and a soft Z. Internalising this plurality, I decided at five that the English language had twenty-seven letters. Under the influence of American import *Sesame Street* and its alphabet songs, I added zee (written with a cross bar) before zed (written without) to end melodiously ex-why-zee-zed. Additionally – and making Roland Barthes proud, although it would be several decades before I read *S/Z* – I wrote the first letter of my own name in reverse as a third kind of Z.

Neither my addition nor my reversal were rewarded, but instead were policed and punished as sibboleths. Yet for my patriarch, pronouncing the Hebrew Shabbat (Sabbath), the sacrosanct day, as a slouching, over-familiar, sleepily sibilant Shabbos in Yiddish inflection was a shibboleth into mainstream Jewish community, one that excluded Sephardi Jews who enunciate their Ts. Had they contrived to stay in Spain as conversos (lip-service converts to Catholicism after the

Reconquista), conversely, Sephardim would have been forced to pronounce 'th' for 's', legendarily a project of Isabella's lisp projected imperiously and then imperialistically into Castilian pronunciation. Linguistic assimilation is a reminder that there are no safe words. For marginalised people, there are many such shibboleths on which life and death depend.

Shibboleth was most recently seen at its divisive work via the Anglophone media's obsession with denying people's right to protest for Palestine's freedom from Zionist genocide and occupation. It was introduced into the discourse by Zadie Smith, in her 2024 *New Yorker* essay entitled 'Shibboleth', where she described statements of solidarity with Palestine expressed by university campus protestors in the US as:

> a series of shibboleths, that is, phrases that can't be said, or, conversely, phrases that must be said ... It is perhaps because we know these simplifications to be imposs- ible that we insist upon them so passionately. They are shibboleths; they describe a people, by defining them against other people – but the people being described are ourselves.

A shibboleth, as Judges tells us, is a phrase that must be said correctly or you will be killed. This is not a passionate simpli- fication or an impossibility, but genocidal gatekeeping. Smith assigns to the students the role of gatekeepers – that is, those with the power to force vulnerable others to speak. But from the moment that Smith was writing the essay, it has been the students who have been punished for speaking what power does not want to hear, as university administrators, cops, judges and now the President of the United States have vio- lated, incarcerated, displaced, kidnapped and deported them.

Smith makes the claim that the students' direct and transparent demands, such as 'End the Occupation' or 'Stop Genocide', are impossible simplifications; this resonates with the powers-that-be designating protest statements as phrases that encode something unspoken, something highly threatening yet also nonsensical. Shibboleth is a useful word for actual gatekeepers because it can do two things simultaneously: it can assert that the speech of those resisting dominance is meaningless, and it can stand at the border and police lisps – that is, the ethnicity, class, gender, sexuality and ability of your body as expressed through your speech. It does not matter what you say, only how you say it, because it is an identifier. To make certain sounds is to name yourself as outside of bounds. To name Zionism, or sexual abuse, or transphobia, or racism, in the face of their structural denial is always to say sibboleth, because to say it is to render yourself in-fans, a person incapable of speaking. To say shibboleth not sibboleth is a form of interpellation: we speak right in order to be named as citizens, to mark our difference from those others who are subject to state violence.

What shibboleth means, at heart, is that violence is a condition under which we speak. As Isabella Hammad puts it succinctly in her essay 'Acts of Language' in the *New York Review of Books*, which, among other things, is a response to Smith's 'Shibboleth':

> When writers (and pundits and politicians) opine
> about free speech rights and violations around
> Palestine they rarely address the material conditions of
> such speech, including the fact that some speech is met
> with violence and some is not, in accordance with the
> unequal distribution of power.

In an earlier essay on free speech and Palestine in *New York* magazine, Andrea Long Chu writes that 'speech has the power to incite action', whether action against dominance or repressive action by dominance, 'because speech itself is already a material act. Yes, anti-Zionism is an idea, not a rock; but if it were only an idea, without any practical potential, then there would be no point in throwing it.'

Chu's rock is a reference to the Second Intifada, (2000–05) often emblematised through the resistance action of children throwing stones at tanks, but is also an evocation of, and homage to, the poet and academic Refaat Alareer, who was killed by an Israeli air strike on 6 December, 2023, just a fortnight before Chu's essay was published. In a live interview on X on 10 October, 2023, Alareer told the *Electronic Intifada*.

> Probably the toughest thing I have at home is an Expo marker. But if the Israelis invade ... I'm going to use that marker to throw it at the Israeli soldiers, even if that is the last thing that I would be able to do.

It was a pen felt around the world. Alareer was a 'key source of inspiration and guidance' to We Are Not Numbers, founded in Gaza in 2015 to provide training and mentoring for young writers. To throw an Expo whiteboard dry-erase marker is to foreground the possibilities of pedagogy and creativity, to signal provisionality, improvisation and the possibility of erasing and starting over. It is a poet's act, one aware of the vulnerability and constant reworking that makes up mutual (s)aid in the face of dominance. A pen is an object that symbolises language; it is a rock and a concept, and that is how it hits home.

What Chu identifies as 'the power to incite action' is the potential expressed in the Expo marker used for teaching:

that speech and writing can sometimes make palpable a space in which we gather together with what we have gathered and share it. Speaking, writing, reading and listening to words that name what dominance wants to erase, repeating them with intent and nuance collectively, can in itself be a direct action because it recognises and risks the material conditions around that speech, including arrest and violation. Naming things together affirms David Graeber's useful definition in his ethnography of 'direct action', that it is:

> the insistence, when faced with structures of unjust
> authority, on acting as if one is already free. One does
> not solicit the state. One does not even necessarily
> make a grand gesture of defiance. Insofar as one is capa-
> ble, one proceeds as if the state does not exist.

Speech has material effects: an oracle can be an obstacle. As Sara Ahmed put it in 2010 in her article 'Feminist Killjoys (And Other Willful Subjects)', 'That you have described what was said by another as a problem means you have created a problem. You become the problem you create.' She refined this as, 'if you name the problem you become the problem' (in 'Sexism – A Problem with a Name' in 2015), or 'to name the problem is to become the problem' (on her blog, *feministkilljoys*, in 2024). As seen in response to protests for Palestine and for the planet, the state or institution tries to focus media and popular attention on the protestors as the problem: as obstructions or trouble-makers or aggressors. Yet Ahmed's statement also expands into the more complex suggestion that to name the problem is to wilfully become associated with that problem, to take on responsibility for maintaining its visibility and enacting a solution. In the first version, the institution is naming-downwards, calling you the problem in and of yourself. In the second version, you say sibboleth: you say, 'Yes, I am naming that problem, and I will keep naming it as a problem. I will write it with my Expo marker on toilet doors and placards. I will embody it, and in doing so, I will proceed as if the state does not exist, as if it cannot name me as the problem.'

I learned this by changing my first name by usage at five, a wilful act, or an oppositionally defiant one. I refused to respond to my legal name, and used my amended chosen name in writing and speaking. It was, unwittingly, good preparation for coming out, which is a clear demonstration of how you become the problem, in both senses. Coming out for the first time can be a joyous moment of living as if the state does not exist. Coming out repeatedly every time someone assumes your heterosexuality is not required by the self but by others, and particularly by authorities.

Dominance culture centres coming out as *the* queer narrative. This perpetuates queerness as being only a language act, one that has no status or existence except through and in this constant verbal repetition. Each new social situation, especially one that is professional or medical, becomes fraught with the anxiety of enunciating an aspect of yourself that you know and understand within your own terms, but have to articulate within the expectation of a hostile reception that may lead to your removal or exclusion. Even the best-case scenario in a tolerant workplace or social situation is that coming out will lead to multiple repetitions, which sustains an entire craft industry of T-shirts, badges, and stickers declaring that you are not what you are assumed to be, because the assumption that you're straight or cis continues to be the norm.

That's why I have to repeat, via T-shirts and badges, but also spoken words, email footers, hand gestures, begging and the occasional strop (the 1980s vernacular British English word for ODD) that my pronouns are they/them. What dominance culture insists is my insistence – me being the problem – is actually me naming the way that dominance culture insists on not listening – me becoming the problem. We could live in a world where there are no assumptions about what anyone's pronouns are. Every time we insist on our pronouns we are living as if that world existed. It is dominance culture that resists that possibility, so that the (f)act of repetition shatters the congruence I want to experience between bodily and nominative autonomy. Coming out repeatedly is not something that we choose, but that we are ordered to do: to name ourselves for another.

Every time I come out – as queer, as non-binary, as an abuse survivor, as an anti-Zionist – it is like eating the pencil that writes my story. I self-name in defiance of dominance, but each time, I am naming something that should not have to be named repeatedly in the face of refusal and denial. There is no need to declare oneself (repeatedly), to name oneself, when one is congruent with oneself and with one's community. It is the violent, invasive action of an external self-mandated authority that requires you to identify yourself at its policed borders. This flashpoint has moved from nouns to pronouns, a term that has become a shibboleth: a word that has been emptied of semantic content to become a gatekeeping placeholder for a particular kind of politics. It's convenient to mock rightwingers who say they 'won't use pronouns' as not understanding basic grammar or the word's meaning, but they are telling on themselves, and it is a profound truth. They do not acknowledge other people's agency, or even their existence, and so will not refer to them at all.

Perhaps what they object to is that pronouns are, of necessity, mobile and not fixed. I become you and you become me as conversation turns and turns about. This is called deixis, or pointing, as with an index finger. It is only when we turn away from that mutuality and intimacy that we say he, she, they to refer to those not in the conversation, pointing over there, across the river. Third-person pronouns objectify us if we don't have a right to respond. Being pointed at and pointed *out* is uncomfortable under dominance culture; it comes to feel like a continuous threat of violence, often predicated on having been mis-identified.

It is particularly painful that most languages require us to be pointed at and classified by gender, which is structured into English, although more so into Romance languages, and most of all into Hebrew. As dissident Israeli poet Yona Wallach wrote in the poem 'Hebrew', translated by Lisa Katz for *Poetry International*: 'Hebrew is a sex maniac / and whatever you women say in a feminist complaint ... / will change sexual relations, make them strange'. As the poem makes clear, it is not us feminist, queer and trans people who are 'sex maniac[s]', but the state and its official language, which obsesses over knowing what people's genitals are.

In Hebrew, second- as well as third-person pronouns have an obligatory gender, and adjectives and verbs are gendered in relation. So, if someone were to misgender me, it would be directly to my face when they said 'you', and anything else they said about me. Wallach (who was gender non-conforming, so I am omitting pronouns) was wrestling to become and name in a language that has no flexibility. Hebrew uses the masculine as neutral, as was the case in English until second-wave feminists took it to task. Wallach died in 1985; forty years later there is finally a Nonbinary Hebrew Project, a free, community-based language initiative co-ordinated by American Hebrew speakers Lior Gross and Eyal Rivlin, reframing Hebrew as a global diasporic language rather than one controlled by a state.

Not every language has gendered pronouns: 254 languages, corresponding to 57 per cent of the total charted by the World Atlas of Language Structures, have no gendered pronouns at all (and there are two unusual languages that have gendered first- and second-person pronouns, but not gendered third-person pronouns). A brief list of the more widely known languages without gendered pronouns covers every continent and corner of the globe: Ainu, Aymara, Bambara, Basque, Chukchi, Comanche, Eastern Armenian, Finnish, Guaraní, Hindi, Indonesian, Malagasy, Māori, Tlingit, Vietnamese, West Greenlandic. You can connect far and wide – mostly outside EW communities, notably – without being asked to point out, or be pointed at by, your gender. Gender, after all, is not constitutive of your identity and it may shift over time or contextually, so why should it be a basic part of speech.

Like names, pronouns are a place to think about what language is, what it does to us, and what it can do in the world. In her 1969 novel *The Left Hand of Darkness*, Le Guin gave us a genderfluid people called the Gethenians. In the novel Le Guin used he as the standard pronoun, despite Gethenians moving between genders throughout their lives; they are mostly nongendered unless they are in kemmer, a period of sexual possibility that causes them to take on a gender; they do so interchangeably throughout their adult lives. After being challenged by feminists for the choice of he, in 1976 Le Guin wrote an essay about the book called 'Is Gender Necessary?', where she stuck by he as universal standard pronoun. But in 1988 she added an amendment to the essay, which I have on a T-shirt thanks to artist and printmaker Frank Duffy:

> I still dislike invented pronouns, but now dislike them less than the so-called generic pronoun he/him/his, which does in fact exclude women from discourse; and which was an invention of male grammarians, for until the sixteenth century the English generic singular pronoun was they/them/their, as it still is in English and American colloquial speech. It should be restored to the written language, and let the pedants and pundits squeak and gibber in the streets.

Le Guin uses pronouns not to point at others (pedants and pundits aside, who are usually the ones doing the pointing) but back at herself and her assumptions. A decade later, she will return to Gethen to see it from the inside, rather than with Genly Ai, the Terran observer-protagonist of *The Left Hand of Darkness*, whom she came to see as a prude. In 'Coming of Age in Karhide', first published in 1995 (the same year as the new translation of Anne Frank's diary), Le Guin challenges herself to give the Gethenians bodily, nominative and narrative autonomy, by letting them speak directly, in the first person, of their experience of genderfluidity. Being Le Guin, this means, among other joys, that she coins clitopenis, a beautiful and necessary neologism.

Pronouns, like names, can be prayers for recognition and respect. We want them to articulate our knowledge of ourselves. Names are where we are told we start: they are our origin myths. They carry stories about our family, our heritage, our culture, about their presences and absences.

They are loaded with deixis, pointing at our gender, our parents' or states' languages, our faiths, even the decades of our birth. Like all stories, they are lies, and, like all lies, they tell us something. We want to be named – not problematised, interpellated or commanded – by our names. For them to be sibboleths, spoken in the way we speak, but without the threat of either having nothing to eat, or being eaten.

On the most holy day in the Jewish calendar, there are three things that you do: stop eating for twenty-five hours; read the many, polysyllabic and unpronounceable names of God only with your eyes; and, repeatedly, name twenty-two sins, in alphabetical order in Hebrew, striking your heart with your fist as you name each one. The prayer known as Ashamnu from its first sin (We have trespassed), is written in the first-person plural, and is recited collectively by the community in synagogue. It is strange, as a child and adolescent, to strike your heart to bruising while you name your responsibility for sins of moral corruption and abominations, sins that have been committed against you by another, one who is mouthing the prayer but not discontinuing his actions. Jewish feminists brought together by Rabbi Danya Ruttenberg have offered their own versions of Ashamnu and the related Al Chet prayer for the #MeToo era, which recognise adults' collective responsibility in upholding power structures. I appreciate that, and I stay with and am stayed by the child who learned to pray their own complicity in their abuse, to name themselves a perpetrator and carry the responsibility of asking forgiveness.

It's only when you pass ba* mitzvah that you become fully responsible for your deeds in traditional Judaism, and only then do you fast on Yom Kippur. So, for my twelfth birthday and ba* mitzvah, my paternal grandmother gave me a set of High Holy Days machzorim (prayer books). In the front of the Yom Kippur machzor, she had penned a poem:

> Be a good daughter
> Become a good wife
> Find a good husband
> Lead a good life

The poem, with its definitional rhyme of 'wife' and 'life', is patterned by its four imperatives that all instruct the same thing. It is hard to find an outside to this interpellation, but beating, or eating, your own heart for the sins of a perpetrator can startle you into looking for a way out.

I only fasted for five years. The fifth year, I ripped the covers off my machzor and wrapped them around my local library's battered copy of *Finnegans Wake*, which I read through the services, standing up and sitting down in lockstep with everyone around me. I raised £40 for a sponsored read, but remember very little about James Joyce's grieving opus except that everyone is constantly eating and drinking. The following year I didn't even bother to show up to shul, but went to school, where I ate a buttered bacon bagel on the steps of the sixth form building. I threw it up, of course, because the body kips the pur.

3: CALLING

— possibly derived from the same base as gallus, cock

Every time I have to speak in public, I feel like I'm going to be sick. It's a familiar feeling. I spent a lot of my childhood throwing up: I ate too fast and got up from the table too fast, desperate to escape. My parents considered throwing up a punishment for this desire to be elsewhere, and not anything worth investigating medically or psychologically. In my 1990s adolescence, cover for my bulimia and alcohol-related expurgation was handily provided by mainstreamed *Girl, Interrupted* post-feminism. It followed on the heels of – and subsequently eviscerated – a grassroots riot grrrl culture in which speaking truth to patriarchal power, not least about such negative pressure on our bodies, was encouraged and experienced as immediate, intense and physical. Feminist artists were reinterpreting punk: Kristin Hersh tells a story of an early Throwing Muses gig, where backstage a roadie for another band said to them, 'Throwing Up Mucus? Cool name.' Punk attitudes to scatological and taboo language filtered into a visceral third-wave feminism whose confront-ational attitude was sheared off by a consumer culture hungry for exploitative, abject confessionalism. When every finger in the room feels like it's pointing at you because you are in the spotlight of a culture that simultaneously demands your speech and is hostile to the implications of its claims, then speaking out can feel, in and of itself, like throwing up.

And it can feel like that because of the odd efficiency of mammalian anatomy: we breathe, hydrate, eat, digest, evacuate, and make signifying sounds through an intertwined set of organs and musculature. Anyone who has ever been laughing hard and choked on food or breath, or even peed themselves a little, may wonder whether this is indeed evolutionary efficiency. In insects, the pathways for food and oxygen are separate, but eating and breathing have been connected in vertebrates for a long time: lungs developed as outpouching from the gut wall in some fish, in order to have the best access to oxygen in aquatic environments. In humans, speech emerges as an amplification and shaping of breath in the flexible cavities of the respiratory system, which is intermingled with the digestive system from the orifices in our heads down through our thoraces to our bellies. So, it makes embodied sense that speaking out can literally feel like food or bile coming back up from our stomachs. It's not a metaphor or all in your head: it's one system where everything important happens.

We rarely think of speech as being intrinsically embodied because EW dominance culture associates language-making with cerebrality, and it also hates bodies. Transphobes are not toilet police by accident: toilets, and particularly public toilets, are a reminder that we are needful bodies, and that we articulate ourselves from those bodies. The need to pee is associated with being in-fans and lying down, with having failed to enter into the EW discipline of being upright and uptight. The rights to equity of evacuation and equity of expression are bound up sociologically as well as biologically, recognising the pee in speech. In a very real sense, a lack of accessible, inclusive, safe and free toilets prevents equity of expression because it removes people – disabled people, trans people, poor people – from public life.

This is what makes peeing, and insisting on our right to pee, such an effective and mischievous protest against dominance. When Le Guin finds herself returning to the world of her great anarchist novel *The Dispossessed*, she turns to a character who is only present in it as a reference: the almost-sanctified thinker and activist, Odo, whose prison writings are the foundation of an anarcho-syndicalist society that she did not live to see. In 'The Day Before the Revolution', we meet Odo as an old woman living in a community based on her writings. She's a widow, she's living with the effects of a stroke, and she remains fiercely independent of mind. While embracing the interdependence of mutual aid, she smarts at the young anarchists who treat her

> as if she were some kind of All-Mother, the idol of the Big Sheltering Womb. She! She who had mined the shipyards at Seissero, and had cursed Premier Inoilte to his face in front of a crowd of seven thousand, telling him he would have cut off his own balls and had them bronzed and sold as souvenirs, if he thought there was any profit in it – she who had screeched, and sworn, and kicked policemen, and spat at priests, and pissed in public on the big brass plaque in Capitol Square that said HERE WAS FOUNDED THE SOVEREIGN NATION STATE OF A–IO ETC ETC, pssssssssss to all that!

Pssssssssss to all that indeed! Le Guin's anarchic elder pisses prophetically on the worshipful fixity with which her teachings will come to be applied on Anarres in *The Dispossessed*. She asserts bodily and linguistic anarchism as intimately entwined in their exercise: screeching, swearing, spitting, kicking, cursing and pissing in public.

Women, femmes and other marginalised genders are supposed to neither piss nor speak in public, full stop. In classical Greek medicine, there are analogical associations between the two mouths, the facial orifice and the concatenation of the cervix, vagina and vulva. Speech and sexual activity are linked through this orificial analogy, which is the basis for a belief that they have an organic connection, as if the oesophagus ran directly down into the uterus. 'Now when a woman runs off at the mouth there is far more at stake than waste of words,' Anne Carson notes in her essay 'The Gender of Sound', because 'the image of the leaky water jar [used by Plutarch of a politician's gossiping wife] is one of the commonest figures in ancient literature for the representation of female sexuality.' Under cisheteropatriarchy, the female body is seen de facto and a priori as leaky because it has openings; it is both a jar and always ajar.

EW culture condemns leakiness, and condemns non-cis male bodies by association. It finds what Carson describes as something particularly 'disturbing or abnormal about the use of signs to transcribe upon the outside of the body a meaning from the inside of the body that does not pass through the control point of logos [the rational word]'. Carson links this to Freud's analysis of hysteria as a putting of the inside of the body on the outside through physical symptoms. It was witnessing hysterical patients at Salpêtrière hospital in Paris that gave Freud the idea that there must be an unconscious that is communicating however it can, including through the body.

He also got the wild idea to actually listen to those diagnosed with hysteria and related conditions such as neurasthenia. What he hears, when he asks them to listen to themselves and their bodies, and to their seemingly inexplicable symptoms, is an endless repetition of sexual abuse perpetrated by adults on children and young people. Symptoms that twist together breathing, eating, speaking and genital pain repeat in Freudian case studies. Choking, shortness of breath, digestive issues, bad dreams, suicidality and speech considered illogical or inappropriate are also listed by Hippocratic medical writers as afflicting young women over two millennia earlier, according to classicist Susan Guettel Cole, writing about how Artemisian rituals responded to these symptoms. The classical medical prescription was marriage and impregnation, both supposedly sealing the leaky mouths of the jar.

Freud initially responded by developing the talking cure, which could be described as encouraging further leakage rather than fixing or stopping up the jar. He would, however, later repudiate his own case histories and betray his patients by arguing that they were, in fact, leaky: that they were not survivors but fantasists and even seducers, in contrast to what he had earlier called 'seduction theory', his name for his hypothesis that symptoms of hysteria were the result of endemic sexual abuse of children by adults. In an exhaustive study as projects director of the Sigmund Freud Archive, Jeffrey Moussaieff Masson demonstrated that Freud had seen forensic evidence for such abuse, and that he subsequently abandoned seduction theory not through a lack of evidence, but a failure of moral courage. In the climate of rising anti-semitism Freud faced in post-WWI Vienna, psychoanalysis itself was seized on as a 'Jewish' science describing 'Jewish' neuroses and psychoses, even as its base of practitioners and patients expanded globally. To continue publishing his case histories would have exacerbated a shande fur di goyim, which means a shame in front of non-Jews, also known as washing the community's dirty laundry in public.

A shande fur di goyim was a Yiddish phrase I heard a million times as a child, meaning keep schtum about what happened at home or in community, for shame! I was startled when I re-encountered the phrase after 2016, as used by leftist Jews in the US to call out Zionist, assimilationist and right-wing Jews who were serving in the first Trump administration. When queer Yiddish burlesque troupe the Shmutzik Shmates (dirty rags, aka laundry, in Yiddish) and queer and trans grassroots movement Werk for Peace put a call out for a flashmob to show up 'loud and yiddish to say "Shande Shande Stephen Miller" ... [to] reject all attempts by Miller and his allies to deflect legitimate criticism with false claims of anti-semitism', they fundamentally altered my understanding of shande. I realised that what Freud and I had internalised – or more pointedly, assimilated – was respectability politics, its silencing that feels like shame but is really fear. In a hierarchical society, shame too often names a shallow mechanism that activates fear around a loss of status; in a more horizontal or anarchic framework, shame can name a moment where we listen *through* the fear, such that we can identify and confront what is making us afraid. What the Shmutzik Shmates made exhilaratingly audible to me was how respectability politics, a fear of loss of status, can make us act in shameful ways, including serving power and preserving the status quo. And that itself is dirty laundry we need to shake out.

It is hard to hear through that nauseous fear-shame, and Freud was legitimately afraid. Antisemitism in Vienna was violent even before the Anschluss. So, he listened to that shaming and, in a sense, internalised the accusation that sexual abuse, like neurosis, was in some essential way 'Jewish'. He missed an opportunity to share his evidence that it was in fact structural and systemic within EW cishetero-patriarchy, not a product of a particular subculture or smaller community. Even – or especially – in the face of such threats, it is Freud's fearful actions that were the shande. In turning away from his patients and towards his own respectability, he substituted a vulnerable community for himself.

The third book of the Torah is called Vayikra, meaning 'And [He] called', capital-H He being God. What God is calling for is animal sacrifice, that perverse metaphorical act of substitution that first appears in Bereishit to let a father off the hook for planning to murder his own child. Repressing his own knowledge, Freud sacrificed his patients and substituted his fantasy that they're always asking for it, and if not actually asking, then imagining (asking for) it. He hoped that preserving the status quo by sacrificing children for their fathers' actions would protect him from persecution by fascists as it had from fear-shame. It did not.

Intense feelings, such as internalised fear-shame, can choke us from speaking. While there is no organic connecting passage between the genitals and the orifices of the head, they are all places where inside and outside meet and exchange, and thus sites of both expression and vulnerability. It's not entirely untrue to claim that there are connections that run through our bodies from our heads to our asses. One of them is the spine, carrying many of the nerves that connect our upper and lower bodies – but not all of them. That would be efficient, but also incredibly dangerous. Instead, some crucial neural infrastructure runs down the front of our bodies so that it can interface with all our thoracic and abdominal organs of breath, digestion and evacuation. The celiac plexus sits just below the sternum and above the diaphragm. You might know it better as the solar plexus, so called because it is a cluster of outwardly radiating nerve fibres. It wraps around the root of the abdominal aorta

73

like a serpent or dragon coiled around a tree, an image that appears across world cultures.

This is why when you are overcome by emotions, it can be hard to speak. You are verklempt or farklempt, a Yiddish word for upset or overwhelm that means clamped, seized, gripped. It's literal. When your solar plexus is tensed, the aorta is blocked and your abdominal organs get short of blood. At the same time, the vagus nerve – the largest in the cluster – sends signals to the brain to halt the movement of peristalsis, so you don't shit yourself with fear and/or need to shit while in a vulnerable or exposed position. When you're calm, the vagus nerve, as part of the parasympathetic nervous system, stimulates the digestive organs to relax, release digestive enzymes, and let go.

Controlled deep breathing acts to release or repair the solar plexus, including after what's known as getting the wind, or breath, knocked out of you. It's not your lungs that have been hit (they're tucked up inside your rib cage for protection), but your diaphragm, so you might struggle to speak as well as to breathe. Breath, speech and digestion are all disrupted by tension in, or violence to, the solar plexus. Being farklempt is a sign that our nervous tension is affecting our inner awareness, our ability to listend to ourselves, which is also our ability to listen to and through the world. There are strong indications that the vagus nerve also communicates with the prefrontal cortex, which is involved in regulating the limbic system, the seat of those crucial homeostatic feelings that tell us instantaneously whether we are safe or not.

If you never feel you are safe, then there is no homeo-stasis for you. Once fight-or-flight has kicked in, your body has no way of knowing whether the adrenaline that drives it is responding to a clear and present danger. When someone with post-traumatic stress is triggered, the adrenal reaction repeats in relation to the original trauma, not the incident in the present. You can tell yourself as much as you like that you're fine, but your body is responding to precedent. And it's not exactly lying: it's calling your attention to something you don't want to think about. I learned the word adrenaline when I was seven, before taking part in a school speech day. I remember sitting in the car with my dad, hyperventilating with anxiety and nausea, desperate not to take part. He told me that what I was feeling was adrenaline pumping around my body, and that adrenaline was good for me, because it would keep me sharp, so I would win. The effects of adrenaline – raised heart rate, deeper breaths, dilated pupils, higher blood glucose – can be addictive, as they are designed to blot out fear or pain, in order to get your body moving in an emergency. The cycle is hard to break, because the more adrenaline pumping in your system, the less able you are to slow down and listend to yourself.

So, I have to ask myself why I have made it my vocation to speak and write in public about difficult subjects, to be outspoken about sexuality, gender and power. For a long time, I did believe that adrenaline was good for me, and then I believed that I was addicted to its effects. I saw public speaking, as Odo does, as a form of protest against the gendered limitations placed on me, and more deeply against the expectation that I would take it lying down, that I would be remanded in in-fans by the repeated trauma that had silenced me. I do get a kick out of the disobedience, out of using what my grandmother would have considered bad language to lead a bad life, out of using both scatological and medical terminology, and intermixing them indiscriminately.

Out of calling out the Siggies and other bad daddies, out of refusing syntactical niceties and semantic certainties in favour of pissing noisily into the tent (and often the wind) with the kind of incontinence that Carson observes. Yet I consistently and simultaneously feel verklempt: I do not wish to spill my guts as if I were an animal that I were sacrificing. I am called to speak, and live with the fear-shame that the call is coming from inside the house.

Call is one of those small words that expand and expand when you look into their documented etymologies. At first, call is call is call, across many Norse and Germanic languages. And then the *OED* makes its favourite leap to serve PIE at the end of its definition. I also love pie, but PIE – Proto-Indo-European – is a pie in the sky. There is no direct evidence that PIE was ever spoken, but it has come to define EW thinking about language. It was, of course, a British judge in colonial Bengal who formulated the best-known version of the hypothesis in 1786, in the prime era of EW colonial taxonomies. 'The taxonomic impulse is the taxidermy impulse ... [a] love language of embalmed possession', as Tao Leigh Goffe writes in *Dark Laboratory: On Columbus, the Caribbean, and the Origins of the Climate Crisis*.

Once PIE was served, linguistic diversity – like biodiversity – was stuffed. Instead, there were trees of begats and, yes, daughter languages. Why does call mean call? asks the *OED*, grasping. Well, in some Slavonic languages there are words beginning with gla- that mean word, speech, voice (hence Glagolitic script, used for some Slavic languages before Roman standardisation). These resonate in English words like gullet and gulp, and – oh, ED! – perhaps the Latin word gallus, which means cockerel, an animal noted for its noisy cries.

Companion animals eat PIE whole. These persistent, intimate co-beings defeat etymologists' attempts to locate them in the grand scheme of begats. Dog, frog, hog, pig, stag, earwig, teg (a young sheep) and haysugge (hedge sparrow) are all of boggy, unknown origins. Because they are rarely used in Old English documents, the *OED* considers them 'non-literary and informal'. They're what people who didn't have much access to or need for writing actually said of their familiars. My obsession with etymology began with dog: my Latin teacher told us that in earlier times, the explanation for the uniquely English word dog – rather than the Germanic-derived hound, or anything canine and Latinate – was that it was 'God backwards'. Delicious poppycock.

Cock and chicken are likewise somewhat puzzling to the *OED*: possibly related and possibly not, both possibly 'imitative' or onomatopoeic (that is, a chicken's name is its call). Cock, like gallo, the Latin-derived Spanish word for cock that turns up in tangos and street slang, has a gendered sensibility that extends beyond the farmyard to refer to particularly loud performances of human masculinity. Their cock-of-the-walk power pose suggests an uneasy relation to what we mean by chicken in English, a sense of cowardice that references the domesticated bird's inability to fly away from predators. In calling something out, we often experience that same duality of pumped-up cockiness and inner quailing, of going for it and feeling stuck, of being loud in our own words and choking them down. There is a sense that in calling out, we are over-reaching, over-stretching our nerves and chords and muscles, putting outside what should be kept in, kept small.

I remember being told as a child, often after I'd thrown up, 'Your eigen are bigger than your pipik': your eyes are bigger than your stomach, an oft-gendered critique of an appetite for life, such that desire is punitively inverted into fear or revulsion. It's our lips and tongue, along with the ears, hands and genitals, that are 'bigger' than our stomachs, according to the sensory homunculus, an odd-looking image of the human body where body parts are scaled according to their density of sensory receptors. The places where we interface directly with the world are densest, and therefore loom the largest out of Wilder Penfield's drawing. The Yinglish expression 'your eigen are bigger than your pipik' gives a similarly recalibrated image of the body, one with the popped eyes of manga and anime. For me, it was also haunted by the other domestic usage of the word pipik, to refer to the gizzard of a chicken, part of its digestive system. In my head, my stomach was that-sized, a chicken belly scared of food. The gizzard is a small meaty knot that is sold together with the chicken's oesophagus as giblets. Known in Yiddish as gargle and pipik, giblets are served as a choice part of goldene yoykh, golden broth or chicken soup, the most quintessentially Ashkenazi Jewish food. The stomach and throat, the bird's sonic and digestive architectures, are grouped together as foodstuffs, serving up and silencing the noise-making capacity that defines the cock – almost like revenge.

I hadn't thought about pipiks for decades until I read Naomi Klein's *Doppelganger*, which is about – among other things – being consumed by being misnamed, due to the online confusion of Klein and Naomi Wolf, two North American Jewish feminists who became prominent voices in the 1990s. Klein comes by her use of pipik not from her own Jewish upbringing in Montreal, but from American novelist Philip Roth, about whose work she has understandably ambivalent feelings. She arrives at the word through Roth's wrestle with Zionism in his metafictional novel *Operation Shylock*, whose protagonist, a writer called Philip Roth, has a doppelganger named Moishe Pipik, a word that Klein says was a 'catchall diminutive given to naughty kids and schlemiel-like characters in [Roth's] childhood home'. To Roth, pipik meant bellybutton, rather than belly, and Klein sees pipiking – following Roth – as a form of navel-gazing. Pipiking is a bodily word for something that disembodies us, because to navel-gaze means to obsess intellectually, to be absorbed in one's own inner mental world. You could call this having eigen instead of a pipik, spending too much time observing one's thoughts rather than being open to an appetite for life.

For Klein, pipiking means narcissism, but also the outward social effects of such self-centred speech, exemplified by the recursively doubled conversations in Roth's novel between the author's alter ego and the author's alter ego's doppelganger. All speech and ideas become referred back through the echo chamber of the individual, such that the outside world becomes trivialised, and even fictionalised. The outward effect of pipiking is thus to erase everything *but* the pipik, the centre of the universe, such that there is no outside to narcissism, which extends the borders of the self to match and erase the borders of the world. Pipiking feeds, and feeds on, fear-shame, craving what is (falsely) promised by power and its interpellations. The more the pipiking expands outwards, the more we lose identity and purpose, sacrificing them for status.

For Klein, such narcissistic pipiking is what is wrong with contemporary culture. As individualistic behaviour is endorsed by the status quo, it appears to confer power, and so it becomes difficult to get away from a mirroring form of pipiking in ourselves. We either become sickeningly sure that the only way to become real is to assert our egos over the world itself, or else we fall into self-referential spirals of anxiety and fear. Like alter-ego Roth in the face of Pipik, we believe in the monstrous projections generated by our fear-shame, and become unsure that *we* are real. That sense of unreality, and its depleting effect on our ability to name ourselves individually and collectively, is at the heart of Klein's book. In placing the pipik in the centre, she offers us a way out of pipiking. If we can apprehend ourselves pipiking, then we could develop an awareness that pipiking cuts us off from our intuition, what is called vernacularly our gut instinct – that is, an embodied language that layers and interconnects skilled proprioception, emotional intelligence, access to our own memories, and interpersonal awareness.

Listending to our own gut is the opposite of what Klein calls pipiking: we need to differentiate between selfish navel-gazing that is disembodying, paranoid, egotistical and status-driven, and an attuned awareness, through our bodies, of our environment and our connections to others. Gut instinct, with its neural feelers radiating out to what we're breathing, swallowing and eating, is a conduit to shared being, something that could stop us from narrowing in on ourselves until we are our only frame of reference. When we are told repeatedly that our eigen are bigger than our pipiks, when the pain and nausea that we feel are dismissed as delusional or narcissistic, we shrink ourselves and our understanding into fear-shame, clamping down on our connectedness. We suppress our instinctual reptilian processing of (bull)shit, and our ability to call it out and call back.

Having grown up among liars, I simultaneously have a low tolerance for bullshit and a high degree of self-doubt, a terrible combination that means I am constantly stressed by self-gaslighting, resulting in the most-Ashkenazi-possible symptom, acid reflux. My pipik reacts, but I am slow to process what it tells me. As Toni Morrison famously said in her keynote speech at Portland State in 1975:

> the function, the very serious function of racism, is distraction. It keeps you from doing your work. It keeps you explaining, over and over again, your reason for being. Somebody says you have no language and you spend twenty years proving that you do.

Pipiking has a serious function, which is to dis-tract you: to cause you to lose traction and focus, by causing you to tense your digestive and respiratory tracts such that you lose contact with their sensations and the information that comes from them. To be dis-tracted is to be disembodied, extracted from your gut instinct and sense of self. This, as Morrison says, is serious. It keeps you from yourself; this begins, as she states, in insisting that 'you have no language' – that you are a barbarian, a babbler, a baby, in-fans – even after 'you spend twenty years proving that you do'.

Morrison's speech is often quoted, and it's worth observing her in the details of combatting that distraction. Before she did so as a Nobel Prize–winning published writer, she was a comrade-in-palabrarmas to writers as a literary editor at Random House, where, among other books, in 1974 she published her friend Angela Y. Davis's *An Autobiography*. To do so, she faced down a reader's report that called for less 'jail stuff' and more romantic confessionalism. Morrison points out that in calling its respectability politics 'humanness', the report uses 'a word white people use when they want to alter an "uppity" or "fearless"' Black person. Morrison writes that Davis 'does not tuck her politics away. Never. Not even in her dreams. Not in the bathtub. Not on the toilet. Not anywhere.'

Three pages into her memo to editor-in-chief Jim Silberman, Morrison straightforwardly declares the reader's report (which has not survived) 'wholly useless' compared to her own knowledge and expertise as an editor and friend, expressed through memories and anecdotes that she shares with Silberman. She dismisses the report with the cutting note that its *Reader's Digest* approach to complexity amazes me': she calls out its trivialisation. In counterpoint, Morrison states she will work with Davis on the manuscript to 'introduce some of the risk and joy in her life', qualities foregrounded in her admiring anecdotes. Joy, risk, complexity: these are 'your work ... your reason for being', the reason to make an argument with your life. Davis, writes Morrison, 'risks her life easily – athletically she moves always towards feats that could end in death'. This description connects Davis's writing to her embodiment: the clarity of her writing comes from her full inhabitation of her body.

In doing so, Morrison asserts that Davis's intellectual brilliance comes from her embodiment, defying Aristotelian binaries. In fact, she sees Davis's embodied boldness as an opposition to the conventions of the 'feminine':

> The fact is that Angela is not 'feminine'. She responds to life in a manner that can only be described as masculine. That which we think of as masculine – meaning adventuresome, unemotional, logical, fearless, etc. She is not in any way 'a girl'. If this book were about a man

certain problems of credibility would never arise. The
real question [implied by the reader's report] you know
is why doesn't she think and behave like a female?

Davis is not 'that name', to return to Denise Riley. Morrison's
quotation marks around 'feminine' and 'a girl' mark both
the constructedness of those concepts, and her dismissal of
them. Morrison describes Davis as unencumbered by fear-
shame and undivided: 'There are no two Angela Davises.
One political, one human. They are one and the same thing.'

I wish I had had this memo to hand over two decades ago,
when I was at university. Just before finals, a professor told
me that my (handwritten, we're talking about the previous
millennium) papers were 'confusing – you write like a girl,
but you argue like a man'. This was not a #girlboss moment
for me, but nor did I have the confidence to reject its terms
completely. I wish I could say that I found it a meaningless
statement, but I did not. I knew exactly what she meant
and what rewards she was holding out, and I also knew that
both the meaning and my understanding thereof made me
uncomfortable. Looking back, I feel like it would have been
very useful to have the term non-binary to hand, and to ret-
con, or retrospectively construct, a linear narrative in which
I realised in that moment that I was non-binary, not as an
ability to have it all, but to exit all assumptions and be free.

It was not as if, in exam papers at least, I dotted my
i's with hearts. But I might as well have done. My handwriting tended to sit steadily on the ruled lines of the exam
paper booklets, and had a rounded, open quality, which was
the result of years of bullying that turned my microscopic
secret-keeping childhood scrawl into 'good' language. The
social value of lettering with a rounded, open quality began

in the monastic uncial hand, but became representative of the education of white Euro-American middle-class girls towards the ornamental, decorative, transparent, pretty and obedient – all the things that Davis actively refused. As Anne Trubek notes in her book *The History and Uncertain Future of Handwriting*:

> Those lucky women who were taught to write [in the eighteenth century] used their own separate-but-not-equal hand. In England they did not use the complicated English secretary hands or the various legal hands. Instead, they wrote in what was called Italian hand, a simpler script for the simpler sex.

As Trubek notes, even the masculine secretary and legal hands were associated with scrivening, a low-status role, and 'there emerged a double standard that persists today: the more educated and illustrious you were, the worse your handwriting was supposed to be'. So for me to write legibly and roundedly was doubly to mark my exclusion from status.

What I was being told was: 'Your handwriting, that is your bodily comportment, is like someone trained to be and presenting as submissive – but your use of rhetoric is like someone trained to be and presenting as dominant.' What if you don't want to be either submissive or dominant – at least, without the negotiation of a scene? What I heard in 'You argue like a man' was not praise, although I heard that praise was intended. Argumentum, in all its cockiness, is about being the best by winning at all cost. In the Roman rhetoric curriculum that was designed to produce lawyers and senators, argumentum is the prescribed manner in which to arrange your materials, regardless of their facticity, in order to win your case by exploiting your listeners' impressionability. In the vernacular, argument now means having, or causing, a row, which appears as a contestation on a level playing field. Yet argument, as a concept, is rooted in casuistry, in wielding a professional training to defeat those without access to elite education. That's what I heard in 'You argue like a man': fear-shamed within a hierarchical system to which I was an outsider, I'd sought status and respectability. I had adopted, as protective mimicry, the shallow, showy cleverness that was the debating society – style surround sound of my university experience. It's the surround sound, still, of British media and politics: a pipiking, chicken-playing, cocky argumentation, with the only stakes being to win by making the other person a loser.

To buy into arguing like a man was to buy into false advertising, or rather, into advertising, all of which is false. As a child of the 1980s, I was immersed in audiovisual advertising as early as I was in Thatcherism and hasbara, and it has earwormed me more persistently. I can sing more jingles than I can recite Hebrew prayers or lists of kings and queens. Advertising is the ultimate pipiking that eats the whole world, as Klein pointed out in her first book, *No Logo*. In English, advert means both to turn towards (from advertere) and to turn away from (from a(b)vertere), such that any advertisement works by aversion: it is designed to turn us *towards* its empty promise by using rhetorical trickery to turn us *away* from our ability to listend to ourselves. If we can learn to hear this, then advertising can be its own aversion, its overt manipulation turning us away from its attempt to shame us into pipiking.

Advertising, like argumentum, is a particularly overt manifestation of dominance language. They both make clear that dominance does not just want to keep the power of making meaning to itself, but also wants in fact to evacuate all meaning. I take a vengeful, petty delight (because, like all gods, I am vengeful and petty) in calling such evacuation of meaning anti-semism – or anti-semiotism if you're feeling fancy. Dominance language is both asemic – meaningless – and anti-semic – an enemy of meaning. As M. Gessen wrote in their essay 'The Putin Paradigm' in 2016 for the *New York Review of Books*:

> Both Trump and Putin use language primarily to communicate not facts or opinions but power: it's not what the words mean that matters but who says them and when ... With a president who lies in order to demonstrate power, fact-checking is indeed useless if it's the entire story. The media have to find a way to tell the bigger story – the story about the lies rather than the story of the lies; and the story about power that the lies obscure.

The lies are a distraction. What they make clear is that to have power means you can say absolutely anything – meaning nothing at all – and people have to listen and quail with fear at its very meaninglessness.

The paradigmatic example of this in UK politics could be referred to as 'David Cameron's doo-doo', the little ditty he sang to himself after resigning in 2016, as he walked away from having completely ballsed-up the Brexit referendum with no impact on himself. 'Doo-doo,' he sang on mic as he turned his back on the TV cameras outside Downing Street. It's a phrase that evokes both the farmyard cock-a-doodle and the child's toilet time, quite literally voicing bullshit.

Not a contrast to his previous statements, but a continuation of them, it was also a marker that he no longer had to dress his asemic, anti-semic crowing up in argumentum.

I call dominance language anti-semic because, as Gessen points out, its point is that it has no meaning, no significance, except the feelings that the triggered listener pours into it. It has three tones: seagull, dogwhistle and mosquito alarm, which correspond to claim, promise and threat. Seagulling sounds out the screeching surface loudness of dominance language, which is not just physically overwhelming but also a territorial claim. I take its name from the pipiking seagulls in *Finding Nemo* (Andrew Stanton, 2003), who very loudly say nothing but 'Mine! Mine!' Even before the loudhailers, helicopters and sirens that weaponise our vulnerability to sound, the volume, narcissism and egotism of voices in the political arena operate together as an attack that causes us to tense up and silence ourselves.

Beneath the onslaught, though, are the two subtler tones that carry the effective and affective import. The dogwhistle is a configuration of clichés and tropes that assures a particular privileged group that their violence is legitimate and will be rewarded, a configuration that is supposed to be inaudible to those outside the privileged group. The promise (you can do violence) also encodes a threat (others will be subjected to violence), a higher-pitched tone that I call the mosquito alarm, after the high-pitched (17.5–18.5 kHz) electronic devices used by some business owners to torture and terrorise teenagers who have dared – in the increasing absence of commons, public parks, youth clubs, or other free and safe spaces – to be near their places of business. Because of its high frequency, this noise is not audible to hearing adults; similarly, the threat that is the base layer of dominance language is not audible to those with privilege, or its audibility is shaped by anti-semism to be plausibly deniable. Phrases such as 'Make America Great Again' or 'You must remember what Amalek has done to you' or 'A woman is a woman' mean nothing except violence, including the violence of evacuating meaning.

As Alaa Abd el-Fattah wrote for *Mada Masr* from Tora Prison in March 2017, two years into his third prison sentence, 'The authorities have decided: meaning is dangerous, defending it is a crime, and its proponents are enemies ... It's over. We have been defeated, and meaning has been defeated with us.' Abd el-Fattah is referring to unfolding oppression by the Sisi government in Egypt, which in November 2016 passed a law 'effectively eliminat[ing] independent human rights work' in the country, according to Human Rights Watch.

Yet, as Abd el-Fattah continues, the constriction of the immediate situation becomes a cue to look and speak outwards:

> just as we were – in every step – affected by the world and affecting it, so was our defeat both a symptom and a cause of a wider war on meaning, a war on the crime of people searching for a supranational public sphere where they might find intimacy, exchange, communication, even quarrels, that allow a common understanding of reality, and multiple dreams of alternative worlds.

As well as being a writer, Abd el-Fattah is a software developer; with his wife Manal Bahey El-Din Hassan, he created the first Arabic-language blog aggregators with no content restrictions. Emerging from a supranational, radical vision of digital democracy, he remains committed to the internet as a public sphere rather than a pipiking machine, one that can expand access to the 'intimacy, exchange, communication ... and multiple dreams of alternative worlds'.

The internet is only the latest in millennia of communications technologies, stretching back long before verbal language, in which we have shared and exchanged intimacies and imaginings. Dominance culture polices histories of communication, whether by commission, such as censorship, or by omission, such as the *OED*'s focus on written sources. This means the intimate and imagined are often hard to trace, such that we have to reinvent or recover them over and over. When they are recorded, it is in such community-sourced projects as Marwan Kaabour's deeply unofficial *The Queer Arab Glossary*, which began online as a blog called Takweer. What survives of us is what we save. What survives in the official record is what is allowed to be there by the state, which is the enemy of meaning.

The official record goes beyond tablets of stone and scrolled decrees and the Magna Carta behind hammer-proof glass. In his compendious work on linguistics, *How to Kill a Dragon*, celebrated philologist Calvert Watkins suggests that – just as much as legal codes – epic and praise poetry were part of the official record, and functioned as key vehicles for the evolution and spread of Indo-European languages. These officially sanctioned and rewarded poems could and did travel from place to place in a way that legal codes did not. Poetic language, Watkins reasons, transmits the etymologies that stretch back from Old Irish to Sanskrit and into the distant mists of PIE. With formidable acumen, he traces not just lineages of words, but also shared grammatical and even sonic structures that repeat across three millennia of foundational texts, spanning more than a continent, from Old

Hittite texts of the seventeenth century BCE to the *Rigveda* (1500–1100 BCE) through the orally transmitted Homeric epics put into written form between the eighth and sixth centuries BCE to the early Irish prose epics, written down around 1100 CE but composed centuries earlier.

Across all of them he traces a narrative structure: the ruler kills the dragon (or analogue, such as the people on the other side of the river who have gold, or grain, or water) and gets the gold; the poet sings about it, and about how singing a poem is very heroic and much like killing a dragon (including beating other poets); the poet gets some of the gold, along with status and respectability, as a reward for winning the singing competition; the approved poem circulates and travels outwards. This is how language memes. The poem's success leads other poets to imitate it, to get the gold. For the win, the official court poets shape, over and over, the sonic, syntactic and narrative structures of the song – its argumentum – to mirror the action of killing the dragon. This takes many forms, from alliteration (especially of killing l's) to certain verb forms highlighted by specific syntactical structures, as well as particular and recognisable metaphors and similes, such as the equivalence of the dragon and the enemy, the other around whose vulnerability and difference fear-shame swirls.

When Le Guin returns to Earthsea in 1990, eighteen years after she ended the original trilogy with *The Farthest Shore*, it is the dragons she returns for. The dragons – and vulnerable, excluded humans, who turn out to have a closer kinship to dragons than the winged beings' magic, might and magnificence might at first suggest. In *Tehanu*, Ged returns to his home island of Gont having lost his power in the dry lands of death. Tenar, now a widowed farmer, has become the carer of Therru, a young survivor of rape and violence. Badly scared and scarred, including damage to her throat, Therru is set outside the conservative, suspicious social order of Gont by her physical difference. Therru was burned by her attackers but, as her scars heal, they glow and warm with an inner fire. At the very end of the book, she is Tehanu, the daughter of Kalessin, Eldest of the dragons, whom Le Guin describes in 'Earthsea Revisioned' as 'male or female or both or something else'. Tehanu, the evening star, 'is her name. It has always been her name', says Tenar to Ged. She is one of the dragonhumans who emerge once in a generation; almost destroyed by humans, she has lost touch with her dragon being.

It is only in the very last *Earthsea* book, *The Other Wind*, published a decade later (with Watkins's book falling precisely in between *Tehanu* and its sequel), that Tehanu transforms, when she goes to the dry land where Ged had lost his magery. Tehanu unbuilds the wall there to free the dead and give the otherland of imagination and spirit back to the dragons. She flies on the other wind with her sister Orm Irian, another dragonhuman, wilful daughter of an abusive father, who had first appeared in 'Dragonfly', published interstitially between the two novels. Orm Irian and Tehanu follow Tenar in their liberation from dominance. 'There is a kind of refusal to serve power that isn't a revolt or a rebellion,' writes Le Guin in the afterword to *Tehanu*, 'but a revolution in the sense of reversing meanings, of changing how things are understood'.

To kill the dragon is to kill the body that is the conduit of intimacy and imagination, to split ourselves because of fear-shame. Writing can be killing the dragon to win status – or it can be feeling the fire that reddens our scars. Vocation, which means calling, gets bound up by pipiking with claims to specialness and status, when it could name a form of solidarity Call it call-and-responsibility. In *Parting Ways: Jewishness and the Critique of Zionism*, Judith Butler asks how they can advocate for Jewish anti-Zionism without recourse to the idea of specifically or specially Jewish values. They write that 'equality, justice, cohabitation, and the critique of state violence can only remain Jewish values if they are *not* exclusively Jewish values'. A vocation is a calling to call out of ourselves, not because any one of us is special, but because we are here together. Each of us is a being in the world, and not a singular being but, by being embodied, embedded. Each of us inhabits a body, where – however sickening it feels as we do it – a serpentine nerve cluster wants to unwind, breathe fire and roar.

4: CRYING

— wail, scream, lament, from quirītāre, originally
(according to Varro) to implore the aid of the
Quirītes or Roman citizens

Sometimes it's what you don't say that leaves you feeling heard, while what you say has you feeling silenced. You are told that crying won't help, while not being told that to cry means, at root, to ask for help. The body cries out while the mouth pays lip service, complicit in anti-semism, as if that will save your life. Spoiler: it does not.

One of the more abstract yet insidious manifestations of Zionism in my childhood was the edict that I pray for the Messiah, Moshiach in Hebrew. If you have seen Hasidim at pro-Palestine, anti-genocide protests, Messianism helps to understand why, and why you should be wary of them. They do not believe in the State of Israel, but merely because it has not been magically delivered by Moshiach. Moshiach will come because they are praying. When Moshiach comes, Palestinians will be removed by the divine being so that the Chosen can inhabit the land. (This is also what Christian Zionists believe about their so-called Second Coming.) I was instructed to make the coming of Moshiach a dominant and continuous part of my everyday life and thought. One of my schoolfriends liked to interrupt games of Monopoly with a loud round of a song that went: 'We want Moshiach, we want Moshiach now!' It was psychically as well as socially impossible for me not to sing along. Like breathing, although I wanted to be dead, I sang although I wanted to be silent, a singing that silenced anything I could speak in the face of inexorability. The end.

I knew that the whole meaning I had been given for my existence was to bend it towards the coming of Moshiach; the existence of my self, my community, of history, was all arcing towards the moment that would make sense of it. I knew. And I sang. And I felt sick. And I crossed my fingers behind my back.

I wish, from the vantage point of four decades and much unlearning, that I could claim I was a primary school anti-Zionist, waging fierce protests against my wraparound Zionist education, which took place seven days a week, at school, synagogue and Sunday school (cheder). I wasn't. There was nothing either political or heroic about crossing my fingers: it was an act of fear. Fear of being transported to a country that I had never visited, where I didn't belong, and where I'd be trapped – for eternity – with my father and the community that upheld him. A place where, given my extremely non-expert Hebrew, I could neither speak nor be heard. It was a selfish gesture, and I knew it at the time, but I knotted my fingers until they ached. And I kept singing.

I knew that I alone, me, myself, was responsible for the failure of Moshiach to come, and I carried it with me as existential guilt. It was more bearable to feel guilty for betraying everyone I knew than to feel vulnerable in myself. Who would not claim that their language acts, whether verbal or embodied, can make a difference, even if that difference convicts them of a crime. The alternative is acknowledging that, in a pervasively anti-semic environment, your words are liable to go entirely unheard. It was, and continues to be, more bearable to believe that it was entirely my fault than that I had no agency at all. I am speaking about Moshiach and I am speaking about the abuse: about not being saved and not being saved. They are entwined, as my fingers were. I did not believe Moshiach could save me, but I had to believe that my words had power. That is: that I could somehow save myself.

This is difficult to say, because it is blasphemy. As in Smith's invocation of shibboleth, blasphemy is when things simultaneously mean too much, mean anything but themselves, and mean nothing at all. Calling something blasphemy imputes at once that it's so meaningful it could bring down God, but also that it's meaningless babble that demonstrates its speaker is outside the social order. Blasphemy as a word and an idea comes from classical Greek, and particularly from Athenian legalese; there are far more records of it being used by orators than by poets. It referred to a criminal act of harmful speech, particularly libel, slander or defamation. This technical term then makes its way into the New Testament's Koine (common) Greek, where it is used specifically to refer to speech that is against the divinity, a usage that had only previously appeared in Plato.

Classical Athens is commonly thought of as a secular democracy; it was not. According to *Eumenides*, the closing play of Aeschylus's trilogy *Oresteia*, its justice system was founded by the goddess Athena, and was guaranteed by the titular Kindly Ones. Before Athena's intervention, they were Erinyes, the Furies, traditional guardians of kinship justice preceding any formal legal system. In that role, they had been pursuing Orestes for the murder of his mother, Clytemnestra, a crime that he freely admitted. Athena then invents the criminal trial, bringing together a group of Athenian citizens to judge Orestes. Facing a hung jury, Athena uses her deciding vote as judge to acquit Orestes. She accepts the argument by his defence lawyer Apollo that only paternity counts, not maternity. Clytemnestra and Orestes are therefore not strictly blood kin, and thus the murder doesn't fall under the Furies' purview.

On the one hand, a cycle of blood vengeance is ended by the formation of civil-society instruments for impersonal justice, which will eventually lead, if we accept EW narratives, to international human rights law. On the other, mother? Fuckers. Orestes murdered Clytemnestra because she murdered Agamemnon because he sacrificed Iphigenia, his oldest daughter, so he could go and fight the Trojan War. Seems very much like an open-and-shut case of Agamemnon started it. And yet it is his murder that is held up as unjust, and in fact as the originary injustice. Patriarchy and its violence are written into the foundations of state justice when Athena, always the good daughter of Zeus's forehead, shifts the meaning of kinship justice to honour the father and/as the state – and, behind them, the father god. Aeschylus makes very clear that the deciding vote in an Athenian jury trial is held by the gods; this may not mean a literal intervention in every case, but rather indicates an internalisation by every citizen called to serve, Athenian-born male property-owners only. While blasphemy, in Athenian legal discourse, is a charge against those who critique humans who hold power, what is lurking behind those humans is a divine pantheon that is insulted by challenges to the social order.

Blasphemy's etymology is more mysterious than its semantic trajectory. The -phemy bit means speaking, but the blas- bit is unexplained. One strong suggestion is a relation to the Greek verb blaptw- (blaps- in past tenses), which means to harm, ranging from impede or trip to degrade, violate or despoil. In rhetoric, it can mean to detract from or undercut. Like blaptw-, blasphemy imputes harm, the severity of which is dependent on how seriously you take dominance, and how seriously dominance takes itself: it can range from a lively irreverence to a death-sentenced impiety, with the serious effects of libel in between. Blasphemy's invocation of divine power is a reminder that litigious systems favour the already powerful. Dominance takes away from us both the right to criticise, and the right to not be insulted, as facets of its power. So, we cannot speak about harms: there is no equivalent word to blasphemy that refers to the harmful lies told downwards by power.

What there is, is the word blame, which is in fact the word blaspheme. There's not a complicated mechanism by which blaspheme becomes blame: French blasphemer sheds consonants to blasmer, then blamer, as if even saying the word is so dangerous that you cross your fingers by not giving a ph. This seems contradictory, but it rolls off the tongue more easily: blame, a secular fingerwag whose circular logic (think of the three Spideys pointing at each other) hides its backing by a higher power. Were there no power that we were afraid of being struck down by, we would not blame ourselves.

We blame ourselves, as we shame ourselves, for daring to breach the dominant social order. My crossed fingers were a sign that I knew that if I cried out, I would be in the wilderness, that displaced place that is associated with the unheard voice. According to Rabbi Danya Ruttenberg, 'midbar, wilderness/desert, and the word "speak", midaber, have the same root d-b-r', leading 'to much wordplay over the years' in rabbinical tradition. The wordplay particularly relates to the title of the fourth book of the Torah, Bamidbar, which means in the desert; the fifth book is called Debarim (also written Devarim), meaning words, and the echo is right there. Bamidebarim. Bamidbar stands out because it's the only book whose first word does not appear to refer directly to language and speech; even the first, Bereishit (meaning in the beginning), is wittily the word that comes before the Word. So, Ruttenberg suggests that Bamidmar means, punningly, not just the desert or wilderness, but the voice that cries out there: the voice associated with prophecy, which has the strange quality of coming directly from God, and yet being unheard (or at best misheard) by humans, especially those with power, who often consider prophecy to be blasphemous.

Prophecy's awfulness is that it must go unheard and condemned before it can be apprehended, which often only occurs belatedly, after the terrible thing comes true. This means that truth-telling is proclaimed to be lying, such that prophecy is heard as blasphemy. Prophecy is not just saying something unpopular or unpalatable, nor does its frisson lie in its prediction. To see prophecy as 'I told you so' loses the significant strangeness of a speech act that is accepted to be divinely inspired, yet also necessarily disbelieved and disparaged.

Prophecy often appears as different or disordered speech, and this is given as a cause for disbelief. Its deliverers are those who are not considered speaking subjects or rational actors, such as asses, rocks, serpents, women and those who cross gender boundaries like Tiresias, a prophet who struck a snake and was turned into a woman, and then back into a man after seven years. They speak blasphemously on their own terms, terms that flow into them from the outside, and then flow out of them to put their insides – ravaged by divinity – on the outside. In *Inventing the Barbarian: Greek Self-Definition through Tragedy*, Edith Hall notes that the prophet Kassandra is a rare character in extant Greek tragedy to be identified, in *Agamemnon*, the first play of the *Oresteia*, as not speaking Greek (she is Trojan). Yet when she prophesies, she does speak this language that is not hers, foreseeing her own imminent murder by Clytemnestra, along with that of Agamemnon, her enslaver. Blaming her otherness, the Chorus initially claim that they cannot understand her words, although once she asks them, 'Am I a prophet of lies? Just babbling' (line 892 in Anne Carson's translation), the Chorus state that they understand, and therefore believe her.

She convinces the Chorus to believe her like a brilliant detective, naming the unspoken crimes committed by Clytemnestra behind closed doors. She prefaces her revelations in terms that both resonate with and reverse Grimm's ideas about lying brides, in Carson's translation of lines 879–80 and 884:

> No longer now from veils like some firstblush bride
> shall my oracle glance...
> No more riddles.

In believing her, the Chorus breaks the curse that Apollo placed on Kassandra after he raped her, giving her the 'gift' of true prophecy that no one would believe. Aeschylus is playing with his original audience, who cannot disbelieve Kassandra because, knowing their city-state's foundational myths, they would already have known that she speaks the truth, and that what she says must come to pass for Athens to become what it is. Listen to the tense shifts as Kassandra ends by proleptically singing her own funeral song, knowing what will happen after she is dead, in Carson's translation of lines 989–91:

> I speak as one about to die:
> there will be other deaths in consequence of me, a
> > woman then a man.
> Remember what I was.

Kassandra's speech is illuminated with the weird lightning of speaking to an audience about a future which they know has come to pass.

Prophecy takes place in this unusual temporality, which Le Guin uses to open her carrier bag of a science fiction novel, *Always Coming Home*. It begins: 'The people in this book might be going to have lived a long, long time from now in Northern California.' In her creative writing guide, *Steering the Craft*, Le Guin identifies the verb phrase 'might be going to have lived' as being the 'active voice, progressive conjugation, potential mood, present tense, third-person plural of go inflecting the past infinitive of live'. Prophecy speaks from this inflection: this thing might be going to have happened a long, long time from now. Yet it is rarely believed because, in implying flux, change and mutability, the potential mood upsets potentates. Prophecy's potency lies in its invitation to envision not only that something bad might be going to have happened, but also that it is possible that someone or something might be going to have witnessed and survived it.

Usually associated with the future, prophecy is importantly active, progressive and present: in its potential mood, it makes space for us to hear that we could listen and act *now*. But the curse of prophecy has another twist: by believing Kassandra, the Chorus break Apollo's curse, yet for her words to merit their belief, what they prophesy has to come to pass. Kassandra's words can speak nothing into being except themselves, against all the forces arrayed to silence her. They do not *make* the future come to pass, but rather document it from its own future, in which no one will be going to have taken action to save her. They stand as testimony and ask us to attend to our own agency. This is the opposite of the dominance fantasy inherent in what linguist

J. L. Austin named 'performative utterances' – a fantasy that Austin shares with wizards and captains and queens, of a rare kind of speech that actually makes it so.

Austin's most famous example of performative language is: 'I now pronounce you man and wife.' The spoken formula, however, does nothing, not without you signing a marriage schedule at the very least, and acquiring certificates and (wife you) a new passport. The authority in the spoken words does not come from their utterance, but from what stands behind the utterer: 'by the power vested in [them]', which is the state, which is God. The same is true, even, of shouting 'Fire!' in a crowded theatre: people are far more likely to agree to take relevant action if you are wearing a steward's tabard or similar indicator of the power vested in you.

Performative utterance depends on the wearing of power vests, often literal, from priest's robes to police uniforms to hi-vis jackets, which, despite being signifiers of blue-collar work, grant such authority that besuited middle-class politicians like to don them frequently. The original power vests were the robes that bore the urim and thummim, magic stones sewn into the breastpieces, as worn by the high priest of Israel in the era of Judges. Judges is the second book (of eight) in Nevi'im, the second bit of the Tanakh, the three volumes that make up what is called the Hebrew Bible in English. Nevi'im comes after the Torah and before Ketuvim (TaNaKh: it's an acronym). Ketuvim means 'writing', which is a way of saying 'miscellaneous'. Nevi'im means prophets, and its second half is all about the big, famous prophets like Isaiah and Ezekiel, so it's maybe unsurprising that even Judges, which sounds judicial and secular, contains tools of prophecy. The urim and thummim granted a prophetic power, one that enabled the priest wearing the robes to speak directly to God on behalf of the king or high court of judges, and to answer on God's behalf. Somewhat less usefully than a Magic 8 Ball, they could only answer 'yes' or 'no'. This is a precursor of the 0/1 of binary coding: code is a yes/no that can only do what it is ordered, over and over. God or computer says no.

It's irrelevant whether God exists, because the idea of Him is baked into the state, like the words incised into clay tablets in a burned library. And the idea is baked into my unconscious and consciousness, and maybe yours too. I do not believe in God and that does not stop this book being nothing but an impossible argument with him. I remember my A-level English teacher telling us two telling facts about Thomas Hardy: first, that – as expressed in the maudlin poems we had to study – he fell in love with his first wife only after she died and he remarried; and second, that he spent a lot of time yelling at God that he was angry with Him for not existing. Maybe it's easier to argue or fall in love with our internalised versions of people and forces, just as it is easier to carry the blame than to acknowledge a lack of agency.

The alternative to an internalised God is terrifying, in the way that Rainer Maria Rilke said that every angel is. An angel is, at etymological root, a messenger, and this is the message that they carry from a non-existent God: if God doesn't exist, you are responsible for every word that you say or do not say. I cry out, then, in the wilderness outwith both listening and authority. In many of the most common and profound kinds of writing and speaking, we are speaking of ourselves, from our own experience, which lacks published precedents and hard evidence. Where one person gives voice to something that can only be given voice by that person, the genre might be called memoir, autobiography, testimony or first-person lyric poetry. It's an evidentiary paradigm that names the power of the speaker. But in EW culture, it also limits power to that speaker, such that memoir or lyric cannot be heard as a political manifesto, even when it is. Second-wave feminists protested this diminution of the first-person singular, summarised in the slogan 'the personal is political'. This unfolds into a complex recognition that the first-person singular is not generically fixed but can be generative; testimony is metonymic, offering an individual case that exemplifies a structure. In using the first-person singular to root their accounts of a broken system and the need to change it, these forms bear the charge and taint of prophecy, of speaking truth that has a wild energy source but no power vest. That leaves them vulnerable to the charge of blasphemy.

Testimony is supposed to hold both legal and cultural weight. Yet a common colloquial dismissal of rape and sexual assault trials is that they come down to 'he said, she said', in which 'he' refers to the perpetrator and 'she' to the survivor, although what it really names is not the gender norms of rape but the power differential between perpetrators and survivors, who can both be of any gender. What is foregrounded is not the violent and univalent act, but the speech acts of the perpetrator and the survivor. They are, in effect, often the only witnesses to the violation, and this is used to put their testimony into false equivalence – and not even equivalence. 'He said' comes first, even when he says out loud, on the record, that he did it, as with Donald Trump or Althusser or Orestes. His testimony is given preferential treatment; his anecdotal self-presentation is redefined, reframed and reversed to use as evidence against the victim. Testimony only weighs as much as the cultural weight of the body that is testifying, a situation that feminist philosopher Miranda Fricker has named 'testimonial injustice'.

Structural inequality, expressed through testimonial injustice, has allowed entitled white cishet men such as Trump and Brett Kavanaugh to call the testimonies of their victims 'witch hunts'. On the surface, it appears that these perpetrators are describing themselves as witches who are being hunted – but that would be a gendered and classed reversal with which they would be deeply uncomfortable. A witch hunt is, historically, the persecution of the vulnerable by dominance. The actual witch hunts by the Church led to the execution of at least 50,000 people in Europe, mostly poor and marginalised women, over three and a half centuries, from 1400 well into the Enlightenment. Those who could defend themselves verbally were frequently tortured to confession or death: an absolute example of testimonial injustice. Convictions often rested on negative inferences around speech and embodied signification, such as the accused's inability to weep in court, or to recite the Lord's Prayer correctly. Testimonial injustice is even clearer when you hear their accusers, mostly men, voicing such rational and credible charges as that they had had their penises magicked off and flown into birds' nests. That is, the accusers stated that they were hunting witches because they had been hunted *by* witches, and this denial, accusation and reversal is what makes the phrase witch hunt available to contemporary powerful white cishet perpetrators. In positioning themselves as victims, they want us to know that they have been hunted by witches.

When I think about the anti-semic reversal of the phrase 'witch hunt', what I see is myself, using a very large Hilti drill. I am drilling very deep holes in the back wall of the school theatre, leaning my body weight onto the largest power tool I have ever used. The holes have to be deep because we are hanging a bar for a strobe light, which will be suspended over the back two rows of the audience. Before we hang the large, heavy light can, we have to test that the bar is load-bearing. So, I hang from the bar, dangling weightily. This may be the first time in my life that I have ever been aware of my own strength.

We were using a strobe to give power and energy to the play that I was co-directing and lighting, Arthur Miller's *The Crucible*. Focused on the Salem witch trials, it was a useful play for a girls' school due to the large number of parts for young women. Girls got to play all the roles, though, and in the playing, some of us found that we were not girls. First staged in 1953, *The Crucible* was not a play written for a girls' school, although it is often read as a companion piece to Lillian Hellman's 1934 play about a teacher at a girls' school who is accused of lesbianism, *The Children's Hour*. Miller's play was a response to the McCarthy trials and the House Un-American Activities Committee (HUAC), which persecuted members of the Communist Party of the United States of America and anyone seen as conveniently Communist-adjacent, such as union members. Hellman's parable eerily prefigured the experience of queer people working in, and forced out of, state services. While there was some crossover of queers and reds, there was a larger category (and category error) in which queer people were assumed to be weak links who could be 'turned' by Communist spies, by sexual blackmail. Through HUAC, thousands of people were interrogated publicly, with the result that they were blacklisted from jobs and driven from public life – and, not infrequently, to suicide.

Miller testified before HUAC in 1956 immediately before the European premiere of *The Crucible*; he admitted his own brief interest in the Communist Party, but refused to give the names of other members, pleading the protection of the First Amendment's guarantee of free speech. Miller's play excoriates both the hypocrisy of the men who sat in judgment at the Salem witch trials and the self-serving lies told by the girls accused, whose behaviour he characterises as mass hysteria. The courtroom scene accurately shows how dominance's hypocrisy can feed the confessions, true or false, of the subjugated, driven by fear-shame to a panic, which is why we were using the strobe. Yet in drawing a potent parallel between HUAC and Salem, Miller didn't exactly come down on the side of the witches. Instead, he took as his protagonist a man, John Proctor, who refuses to admit the witchcraft of which he has been accused but has not committed, even though to admit guilt would set him free. His defence of his refusal is: 'it is my name'.

Yet Proctor, like Orestes, is hardly a blameless, moral man. Proctor has had, as he admits, a sexual relationship with Abigail, an orphan in her early teens. She is his ward, both his dependent and his servant. Given the power asymmetry, theirs is a relation of coercive consent at best. Abandoned by John, who lies to his wife about the cause for her dismissal, Abigail becomes the ringleader of the accusers. The play rests on a central hypocrisy: Miller takes aim not at the judges who ask a man to perjure himself, but at a teenage girl. Yes, Abigail lies – because she is not allowed to tell the truth of what happened. When John tries to persuade Abigail to drop the charges of witchcraft against him (in a scene published as an appendix, and not always staged), she refuses on the basis that he will never admit to 'fornication' with her in court. He tells her, 'I will make you famous for the whore you are,' throwing her to the ground and calling her a 'mad, murderous bitch'. Proctor may be telling the truth about not committing witchcraft, but he is lying to the court and to himself about his actions, which Miller presents as Abigail's seduction of an innocent, powerless adult man. Thanks, Siggi.

In the stage direction for Abigail's entry, Miller describes her as 'strikingly beautiful ... with an endless capacity for dissembling'. This is what Miller is compelled by, and how he presents witchcraft: as the pervasive myth that marginalised and vulnerable people lie and seduce (which is a form of lying) in order to ruin the Elect, who are Elect regardless of the Commandments and laws they break. The reputations of upright white cishet men must be preserved at the cost of the lives of others, as contemporary rape trials repeatedly show. Thus, Miller presents John as the subject of a 'witch hunt', blameless and put-upon by a town full of hysterical women.

The tragedy here appears to be that women are allowed to speak at all, given that all they can speak are lies. Every night in the school theatre, as I switched on the strobe, my friends, in character and white nightgowns, ran across the stage screaming and arcing their bodies, performing hysteria over and over, as we were not supposed to do in daily life. The words Miller made them speak were lies, but what the timbre and volume of their voices and the contortions of their bodies carried was the truth. The Furies had returned.

Perhaps because I was behind the glass of the tiny lighting booth, I could observe the liberating effects while not hearing the language. It often takes a step back, a change not only of perspective and frame, but also of direction and reflection, to acknowledge that we are being lied to, and being lied to about being to. Visual and auditory shifts can, through mistakes that give us pause, produce truer takes. Of her most famous short story, 'The Ones Who Walk Away from

Omelas', Le Guin notes that it arose from both a reading and a redirection. The reading was William James's essay 'The Moral Philosopher and the Moral Life', which critiques the utilitarian position that the suffering of the few is acceptable if it ensures the happiness of the many, and discusses the possibilities of ethical resistance thereto. Le Guin writes:

> Of course I didn't read [William] James and sit down
> and say, Now I'll write a story about that 'lost soul'.
> It seldom works that simply. I sat down and started a
> story, just because I felt like it, with nothing but the
> word 'Omelas' in mind. It came from a road sign:
> Salem (Oregon) backwards.

Omelas is a prosperous, peaceful society, whose secret is revealed to citizens when they come of age: in a fetid cell, their elders imprison, for life, a disabled child. Most citizens of Omelas accept the utilitarian bargain, but some few – as the title prophesies – walk away.

The story is a variation on the theme that also appears in *The Tombs of Atuan*, that a functioning society depends sacrificially upon the abuse and imprisonment of a child. Le Guin's thought experiment gives narrative flesh to James's abstractions, showing how looking again and looking differently can be triggers for ethical resistance to the status quo. Le Guin's Salem and Miller's Salem both derive their names from Jerusalem, but it is Le Guin's reversal that shows how and why this displaced naming arises through a manifest-destiny trajectory of settler colonialism from the landing of the *Mayflower* to the conquest of the West. Salem O could also be read as Salem 0, placing us zero miles from the witch trials and their foundational violence. Standing close, we have to look backwards, read backwards, speak backwards, to look again differently.

When you speak back(wards) to dominance, there is a prophetic moment of finding out whether your words will bear your weight. Or rather, there is a stroboscopic series of moments, of self-doubt and self-blame oscillating with a determination to feel the weighty satisfaction of having made something for and of yourself, under difficult conditions, at a bodily extreme. In December 2015, exhausted from having lost my academic job, I wrote a long essay behind my own back: by which I mean, I did it fast, in fragments, and sent it off before I could think about it. I sent it on Christmas Eve so that I could forget I'd done so, so that I could write it off like a binge from my alcoholic days, a shameful act. Doubly so, in that, despite being vocally present as a queer feminist critic and poet, I had waited so long to speak publicly and in depth about being a survivor of sexual abuse.

I was very surprised when the essay was accepted, because I had forgotten it existed. I became so stressed about its publication that I committed myself to writing a yearlong series of fortnightly newsletters that would build up to the revelation, both to unpack the material in the essay and to prepare myself for what it would be like to go public. The essay would also be my first publication with a major publisher, in an anthology curated by a prominent editor. For over two years, until publication in spring 2018, I was on fire, reality-testing my own words, my experience of being read, of re-reading myself through the editorial conversation. Only a few months before the book was sent to print, I presented publicly as non-binary and changed my first name. Were they related? At the time, I would have said not. But a few weeks after the editor, Roxane Gay, graciously and patiently entered my new name into the final_final_final_print_this_one.pdf proof, I found myself being asked to make a binding legal statement that made me wonder – a statement that made me feel at once Proctor and anti-Proctor.

Big 5 publishers have lawyers – lots of them. Any non-fiction book from a commercial publisher has been read as carefully by its legal team as it has by its editorial department. It's a form, if you will, of proof-reading: can this book, this essay, prove its claims? It is heartwarming to think that a legal read is occasioned by the belief that what matters is the question of whose story it is to tell, and how carefully it is told, but that is not the case. Rape is already a problem to speak about and write about, because as the survivor it is not, according to historical conventions, your story to tell: you are property. Under Salic or Norman law, rape is a crime against property – that is, against what dominance owns, both material and reputational. Rape, in historical EW legal terms, damages the value of a woman who belongs to a man, either by making it so her father cannot sell her virginity, or by meaning a husband cannot be sure of the legitimacy of his male offspring for inheritance purposes. Like the legal definition of rape, the legal read is about protecting property and reputation: not yours, the publisher's.

The lawyers summoned me because there was a potential threat to the publisher's profits: I am a UK-based author, and UK libel law is globally famous for being a rich person's joyride. Organisations such as English PEN and Liberty refer to the deleterious consequences of this using Geoffrey Robertson's term, 'libel tourism'. The latitude of the law towards the accuser is such that if the libel tourist, wherever they are based in the world, can make the case that an article or book could possibly be read in the UK, then their reputation here is at risk. And reputation is what matters. This is what I was confronted with: the dangerous possibility that a perpetrator (whose identifying details I did not give) would sue a publisher (located in a country where neither he nor I lived) based on his reputation (in a country where he does not live). I had not even given his name.

My defence, because I had to provide one to the lawyers, was that the publication was – in a sense – not in my name. That is, the name on the essay is in every way my name. But it has that import to me because it is in every way not the name on my birth certificate, which is also the name by which the perpetrator would know me and be able to trace me. This had the stroboscopic effect of making my real name (which I subsequently legalised) feel like a pseudonym, a nom de plume, when my birth name is the one that has never felt real to me, and under which I had never published. The lawyers' challenge turned reality inside out in a psychic solarisation, as if I were gritting my jaw so hard that I'd darkened my vision. Livid as a rising bruise was my birth name, and the silenced and obedient fate to which it had sought to conform me. Fading into the background, lacking any status, was the most basic statement I made of my self: my weird, seemingly abbreviated name, which I had made up to speak for myself. Instead, it came to both stand for, and stand in for, my claim to do so.

To say 'because it is my name' would have been to take the traditional approach to authorial authority, as taken by John Proctor. That is, I could have told the lawyers that I would defend my essay's claims with my personal reputation versus the perpetrator's reputation, which would become my personal charisma against his, then the weight of my right to subjectivity against his. If I based my claim on the weight of my name, then, as with 'he said, she said', it would suggest a contest of equals, an admission that he had an equal and opposite counterclaim to speak the truth in *his* name, and perhaps to lay claim to an historical wound as the cause of his actions. This is the cycle of blood vengeance in reverse: the claim that 'hurt people hurt people', used recursively to give perpetrators standing to deny that it matters that they have hurt anyone and instead give primacy to *their* hurt. Power vests will always have a primary wound to hold up, claiming to be victims of our failure to treat them as God. The thing about the power vests is that they cannot be God: they cannot authorise their own speech out of their own power; however dominant and bulletproof they think they are, they cannot be divine, eternal and absolute. The thing they know and fear is that they have no power, other than the power we give them, so they blame us all the more.

Even more than he projects blame for Proctor's loss of power and standing onto Abigail, Miller projects it onto Tituba, the most vulnerable character in the world of Salem. Tituba is the Barbadian enslaved woman who is accused, by Abigail, of being the source of the supposed witchcraft. In Miller's version, she can only gain a hearing – that is, save her life – by being the first to blame and betray others, for which act of survival the playwright and his white characters heap her with opprobrium. One of Proctor's final, supposedly heroic, declarations runs: 'You will not use me! I am no Sarah Good or Tituba, I am John Proctor.' There are those who can be used – poor, old, mentally ill white women like Sarah and enslaved Black women like Tituba – and those who cannot, whose names are their authority.

Miller's repudiation of Tituba was itself later repudiated by Maryse Condé in her novel *I, Tituba: Black Witch of Salem*, translated into English by Richard Philcox, an exhilarating recuperation that makes undeniable the testimonial and epistemic injustice against Tituba. Condé cannot free Tituba from the bind of saving her life by accusing and confessing. But she can imagine for her the full existence that Miller could not, including love, emancipation and her return to Barbados. Condé's novel proudly extends the resistant feminist tradition of speaking back to Great Works – not just speaking back, but, in blending academic French with Kréyòl Gwadloupèyen (Guadeloupean Creole), speaking differently, refusing the power of official imperial languages.

Through Condé's novel, we can rehear Miller's Tituba as a prophet, speaking in the only way that she can, towards a day when she can be heard freely. In speaking blasphemously, embracing the blame and shame of prophecy's speaking-otherwise without recourse to authority, there will be going to have been:

> potential
> > energy
> > > electricity
> > > > gravity
> > > > > power

These physical and metaphysical forces cannot, as Le Guin says of revolution in *The Dispossessed*, be bought or sold. They cannot be legislated or judged, although dominance will seek to de-mean them, to make them impossible to use. They are in our spirit, or they are nowhere. No walls can hold them, so they cry out in the wilderness.

5: NO/THING

— in Norse languages, a parliament, court, council meeting, lawsuit or legal transaction, business, possessions, stuff, being, occasion, time, and (euphemistically) penis

After the serpent, there is only one talking animal that appears in the Torah. Like the serpent, it is an animal that is frequently maligned, although for supposed slowness rather than maleficence. The ancient Near East being an ass-based economy, there are twenty asses in the Torah, and twice that many in Nevi'im, but only one of them speaks: a she-ass, who is being forced to carry Balaam the Moabite to curse the Israelites. An angel is sent to stop Balaam, but he will not listen; instead, it is his ass who listens, and who prophesies. The ass asks Balaam why, given they have worked together for so long, he has beaten her three times that day. Harold Bloom approvingly calls her words 'a universal protest against violence', highlighting this passage in Bamidbar as one of his favourites, and attributing it to the J-scribe, whom he reads as a woman. Bloom follows *The Book of J* translator David Rosenberg in positing that it was J who wrote (down) the Torah's two big, dramatic farewell scenes: Moses handing over command to Joshua; and Moses's death while in direct conversation with Yahweh. The J-scribe seems to have had a particular affinity for scenes of conversation, presenting rare instances of Yahweh talking face to face with humans – or face to ass, as the case might be.

It was only after I exited faith that I learned that the Torah was an oral text, one that was redacted, or written down, by many different scribes at different dates. The J-scribe is considered to be the author of the oldest sections of the Torah. She has that name because, whereas later writers prefer the euphemistic Elohim, meaning Lord, as the name of God, she freely uses the Tetragrammaton, which can be transliterated as Jehovah, as well as Yahweh. This is a big and almost-blasphemous deal. The Tetragrammaton sanctifies the surface on which it is written: traditionally, if a Torah scribe makes any error when transcribing the text onto the roll of vellum, the scroll could not be scraped clean and used again, but – given sanctity by the Tetragrammaton – had to be buried with attendant prayers. I am not supposed to write God in full even in English, as it has the same effect on this page you are reading, such that I would have to bury it for all my typos. I grew up writing G-d, without the orificial O through which God both hears and sees us, and swallows us whole. Oh.

The *OED* is uncertain about the origin of the English name of God: the Graeco-Roman Zeus-to-deus pipeline gives English deity and deify, but God is Germanic in its misty origins. In the beginnings before the beginning before the Word, there is a swirl of terms for ritual practices that refer both to libation and invocation, two kinds of pouring out from an orifice: one of fluids, one of voice, with a suggestive analogy between them as forms of unstoppable liquid emanation. In her aptly titled article 'Pouring Prayers?', classicist Leslie V. Kurke attests that the *Rigveda*, Aeschylus and Virgil all use phrases that mean 'pouring a prayer [as if a libation]', conjuring the projective force of embodied voice.

In other words, an alternative Tetragrammaton could be YEET. When Vine user David Banna filmed himself throwing a CD and yelling YEET in 2014, in the first recorded usage of the word, he perhaps unknowingly reached back to the obscure metallurgical Old English term yet or get, which the *OED* suggests is related to libation-God. Initially it meant to pour; via its reference to molten metal, it came to mean to set or fasten. Yet offers both liberation and entrapment because of the behaviour of metals at different temperatures. This is an analogy for language: it can liberate us through generosity and interconnection, and it can entrap us through rigidity and fixity. Any ritual, any word, any concept of energy and potential as liquid and mutable, can be cast into a thing. And any reified ritual, word or concept, even God, can be liberated – from its binds, and from itself.

In Greek, the final Book of Moses is called Deuteronomy, or second law, a very Baudrillardian mistranslation inventing a law that does not exist (as if the Bible needs more of them) from a phrase in the Hebrew that means 'copy or duplicate of the law'. In Biblical Hebrew, the title of the final book of the Torah is simply Devarim, meaning both words and things. When Modernist poet William Carlos Williams said 'No ideas but in things' – in wheelbarrows, in plums – he was calling for a vernacular, observational poetry that refused the rhetorical and metrical fixity of European verse, in which words had become emblems of versifying, disconnected from aliveness and change. While admiring Williams' poetics, I am going to call the phenomenon that characterises dominance th(e)-ing. It's a tribute to my most common experience of semantic satiation, the phenomenon whereby repetition causes a word or phrase temporarily to lose meaning for a user or listener. The more I hear the word thing, the more I hear it as a verb, the-ing, meaning to objectify, to make a being into a thing.

Such satiation is a key mode of dominance's evacuation of meaning. Politicians define their public personae by repeating catchphrases deliberately to obtain this empty effect, reducing language to a hashtag that fits on a baseball cap. Whether #change or MAGA, it is satiation as well as abbreviation that generates anti-semism. Such satiation can cause us (especially those of us with cPTSD) to freeze in our speech, among other aspects of embodiment. Oh, I am being the-ed: the thing about being a thing is that it is to be nothing, or rather no-being, to be zeroed out by being pointed out. The more I am caught up in dominance language, the more I feel disconnected and objectified – the more I languish with a longing anguish over the separation effected by dominance. In the semi-rhyme of language and languish, something happens, though, that unfreezes. Language play such as rhyming, alliteration, metre and puns can call our listening attention to ourselves.

There is another book inside this book that is entirely about and made of puns. In *The Emperor's New Mind*, mathematical physicist (and nephew of Surrealists Roland Penrose and Lee Miller) Roger Penrose argues that thoughts and ideas both arise from and give rise to a quantum superposition of brain states. Puns exemplify this, as two previously unconnected words or meanings come together, expanding our present and future understanding, and also shifting how we recall our previous range of references.

This is why I pay so much attention to the roots of words: not because I believe in etymology as a taxonomy or genealogy, but because the more I look, the more I see how many words are 'of uncertain origin', and the more permission I have to play. Leaving quantum theory aside, puns work by associative logic, and words deserve freedom of association. When words (like people) come together, new possibilities and meanings arise exponentially, and that is why freedom of association has been increasingly criminalised both for people and for words, and why we must and do resist that criminalisation.

Arrest and resistance share a root with rest, from the Latin word stare/sistere (active/passive voices), meaning 'to stand' or 'to be caused to stand': to be forced to stand, to stand against and to stand still. Yet a rest for some is an arrest for others, to paraphrase *Living a Feminist Life*, in which Ahmed is horrified by the invalidating 'rest cure' depicted in Charlotte Perkins Gilman's novella *The Yellow Wallpaper*. In a situation of silencing such as Gilman's protagonist experiences, it feels imperative to speak out. We are commanded to 'speak truth to power' in the same way that we are told not to obey in advance – and other ways of speaking may be needed. As Ahmed writes later in the book:

> Silence about violence is violence. But feminist speech
> can take many forms. We become more inventive with
> forms the harder it is to get through. Speaking out and
> speaking with, sheltering those who speak; these acts
> of spreading the word, are world making. Killing joy is
> a world-making project. We make a world out of the
> shattered pieces even when we shatter the pieces or
> even when we are the shattered pieces.

As an abuse survivor, I have struggled for a long time with the dual silencing of being rendered a thing, such that your speech has no value except self-indictment, and being instructed that it was and is my responsibility – and the only solution – to speak out, speak up, for and by myself, and to do so in words that will be understood and accepted within the limits of argumentum. No puns, no analogies, no body language, no emotions, no swear words, no folk tales, no poems, no macaronics, no dreams, no songs, no speculative etymologies that critique the linguistic status quo, nothing associative that could generate a quantum superposition that might initiate change. It was my responsibility to learn to speak and write a good sentence, as defined socially, semantically and legally, and to trust in those authorities that would then certify my testimony as objective and grant it power. As Michael Rosen argues, 'Writing good sentences is a life sentence. Once we are inducted into it, it becomes very difficult to get out of it.' Rosen wants us to insubordinate our clauses; by doing so, we can recall that both sentence and clause are legal terms.

This is why, even when I am not on a march, I carry as a talisman the wallet-sized Green and Black Cross bust card I was handed by a Palestine Solidarity Campaign steward. A bust card, in case you have yet to be offered one or see one online, is a handy document to not show the cops – except the cops in your head. It is not ID. Its advice on arrest is to be silent, which still feels counter-intuitive to me. It's a reminder that my accountability is to listend to myself, to use my voice only to ask for help in getting free, and to believe that I have a right to freedom. This is what a bust card says (caps and bolding are in the original):

Say '**NO COMMENT**' to all police questions during casual chats, 'booking in' & interviews. At the police station you may wish to give your name, address and date of birth to speed your release. For your protection and that of other people **don't answer further questions**.

Do **not** accept a **CAUTION** without advice from a recommended solicitor. This is an admission of responsibility and goes on the police national computer.

You have the right to **FREE LEGAL ADVICE** at the police station. Duty solicitors don't always have experience with protest law, instead ask the police to contact one of the following [solicitors' firms local to the protest].

You have the right to have someone informed of your arrest (make that the **Protest Support Line** unless otherwise arranged: 07946 541 511). You have the right to an interpreter if English is not your first language. If you are or appear under 18 an appropriate adult should be called.

The bust card democratises information that can be hard to access. In doing so, it diminishes fear, which has been enhanced by the increasing criminalisation of protests – and their demonisation in the media.

While Green and Black Cross, who act as legal observers at protests and marches, cannot alone end policing, their abolitionist stance offers immediate support both material and anti-anti-semic. The bust card, a small, easily reproduced rectangle, creates a shared understanding that we have rights, and that in exercising them through strategies including silence, we keep each other safe. It can be hard to be pulled out of the exhilaration of a march where you are taking back the streets in critical mass, asserting a commons in body and voice and words and art, and make yourself revert to silence. It feels like a self-punishment, in fear-shame for being loud and proud.

The bust card is a reminder that silence, like speech, is a contextual strategy, and that is important because there is no way to speak truth to policing. The carceral state sees us all, asymmetrically, as babbling barbarians whose bad language is a lie. Many of us are conditioned to respond to such policing by proving that we can, indeed, speak good sentences, obedient sentences, out of a belief that there is a line that separates those who 'deserve' incarceration from those who do not, and that line is argumentum. There is no good-enough sentence, because all the power vested is on the other side, as heard in the performative interpellation, 'I arrest you in the name of the law.' Arrest, name and law all surround you, fixing you by reinforcing each other in a circular manner.

The bust card is an interruption, a disruption of dominance and its power to freeze us, to tighten the snake of the solar plexus around our aorta until talking, fast and breathless, feels like the only way to release the pressure. The purpose of such policing is to force us to police ourselves, in order to justify the greater violent repression when we do not. 'Look what you made me do.' That pattern is deep in me, and perhaps in you, too. Carrying a bust card is a cue to sense that the pattern is kicking in, and a cue to say 'NO COMMENT' to its antisemic charges until you can contact support, whether from a trusted other or a trusted part of yourself.

In theatrical or comedy improvisation, it is expected that any new performer entering a scene will offer an interruption that, however tangential or re-inventing, says 'Yes, and' to the action in progress. Under duress, finding a 'Yes, and [I need help and deserve to be free]' requires a prior NO: together, this NO and the yes it makes possible are an example of practising Graeber's 'insistence, when faced with structures of unjust authority, on acting as if one is already free'. To say NO, as you begin to say NO COMMENT, is itself a powerful refusal of the-ing: a core toddler strategy for articulating autonomy. NO is a curt statement that consent is not present, and in stating that clearly, it makes a space for us to breathe. To be arrested is to have the right to rest taken away: the right to take a breath, to gather yourself together and go again. Even when that NO is unheard and unhearable by dominance, it is an act of mutual (s)aid with our self that continues our listending, our knowledge that other ways are not just possible but present.

In one of my favourite photographs of Le Guin, she is dressed like a black bloc anarchist who is nevertheless holding a large, colourful, woven carrier bag. She is standing next to a man (possibly her husband Charles), who is holding a protest sign that says, in very large white capital letters, NO WAR. It was taken by photographer Brian Thompson, in Le Guin's hometown of Portland on 7 December 2002 at a protest against the US and UK's intended illegal invasion of Iraq. It was published by Portland Indymedia and saved for posterity by independent site Takver's Initiatives, which takes its name from a central character in *The Dispossessed*. Surviving as a small, grainy, early digital scan, it is perhaps the only public visual record of Le Guin's decades-long involvement in the anti-war movement. In an interview with anarchist author Margaret Killjoy in 2007, Le Guin said:

I am not a joiner, and I lay low in public (except for stuff like protest marches, which I have been doing for the last millennium) ... activist anarchists always hope I might be an activist, but I think they realise that I would be a lousy one, and let me go back to writing what I write ... The peace movements, very loose and ad hoc, have been fine ... [but] I can't put my work directly in ... service [of organisations], expressing their goals. It has to follow its own course towards freedom.

Across the late sixties and early seventies, during the US invasion of Vietnam against which she regularly marched, Le Guin wrote what are considered her major novels. She published *A Wizard of Earthsea* in 1968, of which she would note in a 2012 afterword, 'There are no wars in Earthsea. No soldiers, no armies, no battles ... my mind doesn't work in terms of war.'

She published *The Left Hand of Darkness* in 1969, of whose beginnings she noted in 'Is Gender Necessary?' in 1976: 'In the thirteen thousand years of recorded history on Gethen, there has not been a war.' She added in 'Is Gender Necessary? Redux' in 1988:

> At the very inception of the whole book, I was interested in writing a novel about people in a society that had never had a war. That came first. The androgyny came second. (Cause and effect? Effect and cause?).

She published *The Word for World is Forest* in 1972, in which a devastating, genocidal, resource-extractive colonial occupation is ended by the arrival of the ansible, a device that can transmit communication simultaneously across galactic distances.

And she published *The Dispossessed* in 1974, whose protagonist Shevek does the research that makes the ansible possible. In her essay 'Science Fiction and Mrs Brown', Le Guin writes that Shevek, a brilliant theoretical physicist, was based on 'a childhood memory of Robert Oppenheimer as a young man'. Shevek, being an Odonian anarchist, refuses Oppenheimer's decision to give research with deadly possibilities to one nation-state. By sharing it freely with the galactic Ekumen so no state has an advantage, he upholds Le Guin's commitment to NO WAR.

Not no more war, or no to this specific war, but NO WAR. Like NO COMMENT, this is astonishing defiance to dominance language and its narratives, what Le Guin calls 'the killer story' in 'The Carrier Bag Theory of Fiction'. It is also astonishing as a two-word encapsulation of the commitment that runs through her entire oeuvre, whether on Gethen or Anarres, or in Earthsea, in science fiction, fantasy or essay. NO WAR and its concomitants are found throughout: no police, no prisons, no supremacy, no dominance language. NO is linguistic anarchism in a single syllable. Unlike performative utterance as understood by Austin, it wears no power vests. It is speech that is entirely liberated.

This is very much not what is legally meant by free speech; as the bust card reminds us, our speech is very much not free. As Fara Dabhoiwala explores in *What is Free Speech? The History of a Dangerous Idea*, the EW legal and political imperative of free speech and a related free press was first formulated in Britain in the early eighteenth century: the peak of both the Enlightenment and the transatlantic slave trade. He argues that the 'free' in free speech is thus necessarily underpinned and delimited by the racial capitalism of enslavement, noting that while 'the rebel colonists of North America ... enshrined its clumsy formulations in their First Amendment – "Congress shall make no law ... abridging the freedom of speech, or of the press" ... The subsequent history of American attitudes is full of unappreciated ironies' – such as that this 'free' speech was only afforded to free men, and generally only those who could afford the expensive liberty of critical speech.

'Free' speech buys its supposed freedom from the free market, which has its roots in free trade. The original medieval term for free trade was frank traffic. Frankish was the Byzantine term for all Western Europeans, although Frankia referred to France, the (pre-Norman) land of the Franks, a distinct people. Frank traffic across the Northern Mediterranean was free from tolls for all Frankish (Western European) ship-owners and merchants.

To be a Frank gives its meaning to the phrase to be frank, meaning to be free [with my words], because 'in Frankish Gaul full freedom was possessed only by those belonging to, or adopted into, the dominant people' (*OED*), based on the model of citizenship in the colonising, slave-owning Roman Empire. To be frank is thus to be privileged. To say 'to be frank' – almost always followed by a normative opinion – is to say, 'I speak from a position of power with no fear of consequences because I belong to dominance culture.' Offered with no further comment: in Norman English a frank (derived via another etymology) is also an enclosure, especially for fattening pigs.

Frank traffic was accompanied and made possible by what, relatedly, became known as Frankish language. Elites like diplomats and business owners wrote their contracts and letters in Latin but, from the time of the Norman invasion to the Age of Imperialism, Frankish language was the Mediterranean trade tongue used by sailors. Lingua franca (aka Franka), as it is more readily known, shed its specific meaning long ago. It has come to imply any form of speech generally understood and shared beyond either geographical or ethnic communities. On the positive side, this preserves lingua franca's history of horizontally shared communicatory strategies that are free of status and authority; on the negative, what it usually names is the imperial dominance of business English and other homogenised globalised digital usages that are free in the sense of the free market; that is, free from meaning; asemic. The original lingua franca was a beautiful unboundaried, irreverent hymn of early Romance and other vernaculars, spoken by those who laboured together, often in difficult conditions. Its cosmopolitan make-up was a reminder both of which states controlled trade, and which poor communities actually worked it: Venetian and Genoese, Occitan and Catalan, then later Portuguese, Castilian and French. Berber, Ottoman Turkish, Greek and Arabic are all palpable presences; although the lexicon is primarily Latinate, the way vowels are clipped reflects Arabic influence.

Since lingua franca has, through colonial capitalism, come to mean something like 'free speech' in a parallel sense to 'free trade', not mobile and mutable but locked down, allow me to share with you the lesser-known name of lingua franca, which we could use instead: Sabir. Sabir means to know in Sabir, so the language is called To Know. As Sabir uses the infinitive for all verb forms, it could equally be translated as 'Let them know!', like 'Iston!', the ancient Greek imperative that is the root of history and story. Or it could mean … yknow. Yknow. If you know, you know, a consensual code for the undercommons, the undercurrent of a form of speech that seeks to evade capture and assist those evading capture. That is how it is used in the most famous fragment of Sabir, with my stadium-chant translation:

Se ti sabir / Ti respondir / Se non sabir / Tazir, tazir
If you know / Then you say so / If you don't / Then shut it

This is, brilliantly, the essence of all languages: they are shibboleths that, among mutuals, keep us safe. But that means keeping others out.

In a non-dominance world, such codes would not be necessary and the play of s/language would be all for pleasure on our tongues. Sabir's infinitives-only verbs, all ending -ir, made it easy to pick up and also to rhyme with inventively: it was made for singing. A constantly adaptive oral language, its vocabulary and structures would have been hard to track by authorities; in fact, the *OED* pooh-poohs its very existence because so little was written down. The pleasure of making meaning together was enhanced by the pleasure of getting away with it, with a nod and a wink. If you know, then you say so, ti respondir: you answer in kind. If you don't, then all you can do is tazir, stay schtum. This iykyk allowed sailors and other mobile subjects to share information, pass on secrets, cut deals, keep moving and get free: a reminder of what we want from communication.

Sabir disappeared under the waves of the ocean blue, erased very specifically by the first published grammar of a Romance language. The capitalised Grammar originally referred only to the Latin textbook that was used across medieval Europe. Latin's imperial and churched dominance means the Grammar is deep in many similarly imperialising languages, as in their law codes. 'Language has always been the companion of empire', Antonio de Nebrija admitted proudly, outlining his plan for world domination in his book *Gramática [de la lengua] Castellana*, the first grammar of a European vernacular for a millennium. Nebrija, the First Chair of Grammar at the University of Salamanca, used the enormous success of his Latin grammar book of 1481 to authorise an audacious grammar of the new language of Castilian, one of many vernaculars in the Iberian Peninsula, but importantly the one spoken by King Ferdinand and Queen Isabella. His *Gramática* marked the precise moment when grammar moved from meaning the structure of Latin and its study to the structure of any (dominant) language and its study. It was published in 1492, not coincidentally at the moment when Castilian sailors were setting off to conquer the supposed westward route to India.

If there is any code that cracks the good sentence, it is grammar. In England in the Middle Ages, the Grammar referred to both the Latin textbook and the Latinate curriculum of rhetoric it undergirded, which gave rich white boys the skills of argumentum. It was not unreasonable to attribute the worldly power of these privileged men directly to their command of the Grammar, and of the books from which it was taught. In the vernacular, any book containing Latin came to be known as a grammar, and the word evolved to branch off as grimoire, which meant a book full of secret language (Latin, or like Latin) that conferred power on its owners by allowing them to work magic. Grimoires cast what came to be known, through a consonant shift, as glamours – a now-archaic word for a transformative enchantment. Grammar names the way that books and Latin, entwined, formed the elite education that perpetuated the aristocracy's feudal grip on power. Grimoire, as a word, attributes that power to occult means, shifting the power vest of authority from royal power, which underwrites land ownership, into mystical realms.

Despite all our many revolutions and acts of resistance, the powerful remain unshakeably in power. It is more bearable to believe that grammars cast glamours – that formally correct language use is the spell that grants dominance – than that we are powerless to overthrow them. Unlike land wealth, language appears, attractively, as a magic that we could grasp and use in reverse. I was taught the modern equivalent of the Grammar by my abuser, and I kept pursuing books and education in the

Arha-like belief that they would give me a ritual or magical power. The more I attended to the working of words, the more I uncovered not magic but histories that bear witness to the material workings of power. Access to the glamorous worlds of government, big business and media in the contemporary UK is still a matter of class, which is gendered, racialised and often defined – but not granted – by education, accent, vocabulary and linguistic registers. If you couldn't speak RP, then you were RIP, as far as the BBC was concerned, well into the late twentieth century.

My other grandma (not the good girl) wanted (like so many bad girls) to go on the stage, so practised her Received Pronunciation through poetic elocution to hide her East European/East End accent. Even though it had not worked for her, she instilled in me the need to do the same: to class-pass by reciting. Listen: 'I must go down to the seas again, to the lonely sea and the sky,' all orotund vowels and enunciated consonants, especially that sibilant final s of the plural seas. I had to look up the names of the poem and poet ('Sea-Fever' by John Masefield), but its rhymes and rhythms remain memorable on my tongue, its taming pronunciation so at odds with its wild yearning for the sailor's supposedly 'vagrant gypsy life'. British maritime dominance depended on criminalising so-called vagrancy in order to legalise press-ganging. Anyone designated to be wandering could be kidnapped and forced into naval service, a law that continues to underpin the criminalisation of unhoused people and Gypsy, Roma and Traveller people today.

To Masefield, however, it is all play: the poem ends with a longing for 'a merry yarn from a laughing fellow-rover'. Yarn is a sailor's word, according to historian Marcus Rediker, emerging from long hours spent on deck, where a multilingual crew would be mending ropes and telling tall tales in a lingua franca. What I hear singing in Sabir is this necessity: language is – mouth to mouth, hand to hand, face to face – a commons, improvised through negotiation and improvisation, a yarn braided to hold fast at need, pulling things in from all over the place because that is where we come from and where we're going. Sabir points to language as a way that we help each other navigate the world, made messily and provisionally, with lots of pointing, nodding of heads, waving of hands, interpretive dance, laughter, flirting and fighting, often on the run.

This is my joyous statement of the famous Sapir–Whorf hypothesis of linguistic relativity, which posits that the way in which we experience the world around us shapes and is shaped by the languages we use. The hypothesis was named after two linguists who never worked together, but independently presented variants of linguistic relativism around the same time. Its multiple, unstable authorship and lack of any authoritative formulation feel appropriate to its thinking about language's mutability. Language changes, and it changes us. It has material effects, as Andrea Long Chu says.

This is why the Sapir–Whorf hypothesis continues to influence writers, particularly in science fiction. It famously shapes classics such as Ted Chiang's 'Story of Your Life' and Samuel Delany's *Babel-17*. It roves across Le Guin's oeuvre, from the power of naming in Earthsea to the confoundingly nounless speech of her late, satirical short story 'The Nna Mmoy Language' – and also her appreciation for 'Darmok', Le Guin's favourite episode of *Star Trek: The Next Generation*. It's a rare episode that shows the limits of the universal translator, the fantastical technology that allows Federation crews to travel galactically and communicate with everyone they meet. In 'Darmok', it can translate the words of the Tamarian language into Federation Standard (which happens to sound like late-twentieth-century white American English), but they do not make sense to the Starfleet hearers, because the Tamarians speak entirely in allusions to scenes, characters and metaphors in their epic poetry. The Federation cannot rely on their defining technology. In a situation of violent threat, Captain Picard has to join in improvisatory sharing with the Tamarian Captain Dathon in order to enter into Tamarian language-thought. 'This is what science fiction does best,' Le Guin writes in her *TV Guide* article on *TNG*, her only known piece of TV criticism. 'It challenges our idea of what we see as like ourselves. It increases our sense of kinship' – and in 'Darmok' it does so through linguistic relativism.

In the Sapir–Whorf hypothesis, language is itself a science fiction, both a transformative technology and a story of how such a technology mediates encounters with those we don't at first understand. Language, like science fiction, can tell itself as a story of dominance and destruction, or it can tell itself as a story of collaboration and improvisation. Inspired by Sabir and its sailor speakers of the wharves, I propose a Sabir-on-the-Wharves hypothesis: that language, like us, is made in and of the world, in motion, especially where worlds meet under dominance and with the need to subvert it. Where movement is not free, a kind of yarning space arises circumstantially and provisionally, and you grab it with your pirate-hands before it is taken from you. Sabir offers a dream of speaking freely not because it is homogeneous and common (the conventional sense of lingua franca), but because it regards meaning-making as a commons that anyone can and has to use. Sailor, sex worker, small trader, singer, sweet-seller, storyteller, sojourner, servant: all can take part in what we can usefully call improvisation. It's a performance that restores to language a sense of embodied liveness and high-wire risk, undertaken necessarily through collaboration and consent to cross, if not erase, borders.

The 'Yes, and' of such improvisation is a reminder that we are the only authors of our own meaning, the only ones accountable for what gets transmitted and translated; there is no higher authority in Sabir, no written dictionary or grammar to act as power vest, only the call and response that tells you that you're making yourself understood or not. Se ti sabir, ti respondir. To say that something is made up as it goes along is an insult directed at children and other story-tellers, so let us embrace it. Sabir was indeed made up as it went along, because it had to be, because it had to work. And it did. It does.

Beyond Masefield's romantic fantasies of running away to sea, Sabir was still at work in his lifetime, being one of the many languages, including Yiddish and Romani, that make up Polari. Polari is a derivation from the Latin parlare, mean-ing to speak; the fact that Polari has an infinitive as its name immediately marks the presence of that infinitive-heavy, Latinate language, Sabir. Like Sabir, Polari begins around the docks and with those on the move: show people, carnival workers, actors and sex workers. Only in the early twentieth century did Polari become associated with London's queer and trans subcultures looking to stay ahead of the cops. Like Yiddish, it has been recently revived by marginalised com-munities reawakening their own occluded history.

It's not surprising that Romani, a language with many local variants spoken across several continents, is also found in the Istanbuli queer slang Lubunca, whose name derives from lubni, a Romani word for sex worker. It was first documented in 1999, but its usage goes back to the Ottoman era, according to linguist Lilith Bardakçı. Bardakçı told *PEN Transmissions* that Lubunca is 'an anti-language, because what differentiates Lubunca from standard Turkish is that it shows us how the Lubunyas' [LGBTIQ+ people] reality differs from hegemonic reality' through sense inversions, borrowings and play. It's improvisatory Sabir-on-the-Wharves through and through. Bardakçı concludes that the 'Turkish language has evolved in this cis heteronormative reality, but if Lubunyas are accepted then Lubunca will be standard Turkish.'

Lubunca and Polari, like Sabir, are what dominance calls bad languages. In fact, what they get called is anything but a language, whether it's technical terms from linguistics such as dialect or creole or trade tongue, or vernacular slurs such as slang, argot or cant. These taxonomies are used to dismiss the people who speak these bountiful and clever languages that are improvised to survive in the interstices of dominance language and its homogenising, colonising force. Such languages are typed as lesser, as if any articulation is less complex than any other; indeed, they are typed as such in order to erase the complexity that they carry, of accent and history and resistance. Their fluidity, which encompasses both geographical movement and linguistic expansiveness, is dangerous to fixity.

The effects of the Grammar shaped and continue to shape the modern world. While Latin and European languages, are often seen as having broadened, connected and globalised, we can see them instead as disarticulating, fixative and erasive forces. Cuban–American Jewish literary historian María Rosa Menocal begins her book

Shards of Love: Exile and the Origins of the Lyric with the publication of Nebrija's Grammar in 1492, and notes that it happened just a few months after Cristóbal Colón set off west across the Atlantic, and also another event that happened that same day: the expulsion of the surviving, unconverted Jews of Sepharad/al-Andalus from the Atlantic port of Cádiz. So many ships departed from Cádiz that Colón had to sail from the smaller and less well-situated port of Palos de la Frontera, one hundred miles north. All three events were ordered by Ferdinand and Isabella as part of their Reconquista and as preparation for their conquistadoring-to-come, with the aim of dominating the land and sea, the thoughts and beliefs that people hold, and the words in which they still speak them. Nebrija's bound codex would march across Spain to secure the Reconquista that had violently driven Muslims and Jews from the country, and would then secure dominance of the Americas.

Menocal argues that the 'great triumph of the Grammar of 1492 ... necessarily entails both Conquest and Expulsions'. Language is not just the companion but indeed the palabr-arma, the s/wordwork, of empire. Language is law, church and state, and the Grammar – both as a structural abstraction and the literal book itself – rules them all. Christina Sharpe encapsulates this in a note to one of her *Ordinary Notes*, in which she makes clear the links between the Grammar and other EW taxonomies as acts of colonial, racist cisheteropatriarchy:

> This grammar of the good is the same one that names
> J. Marion Sims and Francis Galton 'fathers' of gyn-
> ecology and eugenics, respectively ... Good men. Fathers.

To name someone 'father' or 'Father' is always an act of grammar, as Hortense Spillers, riffing on James Joyce, points out in her essay 'Mama's Baby, Papa's Maybe: An American Grammar Book'. It is always an imposition of order. Fathers make grammars because grammars make fathers. It's the only way they can steal power. Fathers, as a class or order, refuse to participate in the vulnerable web of relation that is made through repeated labour, including the gathering together and weaving of words.

Against the Grammar: Grandma. Despite all her poetic recitations to achieve RP, my maternal grandmother never made it on the stage. Instead, she chain-smoked her way through five decades as an NHS secretary, lying about her age in order to work well beyond mandatory retirement. She was the first person I knew to use email and word processing software. She was, as feminist historian of technology Anne Balsamo described her own mother, a computer: a cyborg who took dictation from consultants so meticulously and for so long that she was able to identify and prevent diagnostic and dosing errors. She gave me her typewriter when she got an electric word processor, then gave me the electric word processor when she got a desktop computer, so that while I wrote my 'little stories and poems', I could become employable by learning to touch-type.

Despite being homophobic, she brought home *The Well of Loneliness* from the charity shop at the hospital where she worked. She hadn't read the blurb; she just liked the painting on the front: Gluck's striking dual profile portrait *Medallion* or *YouWe*, exhibited nine years after the sensational publication of Radclyffe Hall's (eventually banned) novel, and considered one of the first open declarations of lesbian love in British visual art. She read the book and found it depressing, so she gave it to me in an attempt to convince me that being queer could only lead, as it does for Stephen Gordon, to being an outcast. She had previously done the same with *Oranges are Not the Only Fruit*. As Jeanette Winterson so resonantly titled her memoir, *Why Be Happy When You Could Be Normal?* Like the typewriters, these books were gifts of practicality, intended to accommodate my queer habits by finding ways to normalise them. As with all of those familial lies borne of survival, her hard work made a wayward space for me to wilfully hear something different as (in the) well.

Many grandmas, of all marginalised genders, are available to us all: the word extends grandmanarchically against patriarchal Grammars, and out through oneiric and associative queer feminist ancestry. The great-great-great grandmother for whom I was named was known as Reb Tsorke, which is the Yiddishisation of our shared name. The first bit, Reb, does not mean rebel, but is an honorific, an abbreviation of Rabbi. Tsorke was married to a rabbi, but people came to consult her, as she had both book-learning and herblore, an unusual combination for a Jewish woman in nineteenth-century rural eastern Europe, one that made her something of a local legend.

I did not hear about Reb Tsorke directly from my great-grandmother who carried these received, fragmented memories through her traumatic evacuation from fascist Bucharest to London as a married teenager, but belatedly from my mother, second-hand and offhand, when I started reading Tarot again as an adult. 'You get that from my side, from Reb Tsorke,' she told me, before sharing the hazy facts that she remembered. I don't and can't know much more about her, except through speculative history, what Saidiya Hartman calls 'critical fabulation'. For me, that has meant archival work that is both complemented by, and akin to, practical-spiritual practices that run counter to the rule-bound religion I was taught.

Tarot maven Rachel Pollack suggests in her magnum opus *Seventy-Eight Degrees of Wisdom* that the name of the card deck originates in a reversal of the word Torah. She raises and lets go the possibility that Tarot has its roots in Kabbalah, noting that while 'occultists have claimed secret sources for the cards, such as a grand conference of Kabbalists and other Masters in Morocco in 1300 ... no one has ever produced any evidence for such claims'. Tarot, in Pollack's deeply researched and influential view, is neither magic nor fixed, any more than language is. It is a practice of improvisatory meditation, a path through understanding of ourselves and life. Tarot offers us both a practice of, and a metaphor for, the way out: a return to engaging and trusting our ceremony of belief and our intuition, expressed through figurative and symbolic language. It is not bound in a codex, but printed on loose cards that can be handled and shared.

The cards have been dehistoricised, often rendered apolitical, and used by patriarchal exploiters such as Aleister Crowley to seek control over others. As with so many languages, in the present there are feminist, queer and trans and/or Black practitioners engaged in critical fabulation to redesign, re-read and reclaim the cards, busting them out of arrest. In the booklet accompanying Elicia Epstein's Liberation Tarot deck, adrienne maree brown writes:

> With practice with tarot, we are liberated from isolation into a conversation we can have with ourselves and that which is beyond ourselves, even when we appear to be alone.

How we work with tarot decks can also be a liberation practice, trusting the messages to come rather than trying to control it all.

Emphasising improvisation, brown reminds us that reading, like speaking, is an associative, collaborative and transformative practice.

Taking accountability for making our own meaning means listening to and for other voices, those that are – as Le Guin says of 'Darmok' – 'all myth and metaphor'. It is a work of undoing that takes time. Reading Tarot operates, for me, like a bust card: it's a reminder not to be forced down by dominance language, not to be arrested from myself and isolated from the world. It is a way of reaching for interconnection and relation, the live wire of radical possibility that means that I cannot stay in freeze, cannot be arrested in doing nothing, in being the'd. I can swing my s/word and say: I am NO thing.

EXHALE

To swear freely is to breathe freely. As Mona Eltahawy writes in 'Why I Say "Fuck"', 'standing guard over our language like a baton ready to strike, is civility. Patriarchy reserves for itself the power to offend, the power to be obscene.' When my great-grandmother was dying in late dementia, she could no longer enjoy her favourite read (Marcel Proust in French, in a beautiful edition with tiny type), so she turned to the equally enjoyable Jackie Collins, leading to the startling afternoon that she asked me: 'What does it mean, to fuck?' I was fourteen and too verklempt by the doubly puritanical culture of my upbringing to offer the simple and reciprocal openness of, 'It means to have sex.'

Swear words are seen as words that can taint the speaker as well as the (impressionable) hearer; children are shielded from them so that they do not repeat them, as that could lead them to wonder at or even enact their referents, and thereby – according to puritanical logic – become sullied. To curse is to be cursed. According to the most recent etymological thinking, curse comes from cursus, meaning the Order of Service in church: on the one hand, it could be that the Latin Order of Service, like the Latin Grammar, was seen as giving words an otherworldly power; on the other hand, it could be that the ordering of prayer and the authority of those ordering it was experienced as a burden, and spoken against. Either way, in the movement from sacred to vernacular speech, curses draw their power from blasphemy. Unlike swear or oath, which mean to curse in its sense of cuss, curse does not mean to make a legally and/or morally binding statement backed up or demanded by power vests. Most of us will only ever do so in court, where the law has the obscured backing of God.

I have oathed in one circumstance only, and that was in the revoking. The first service of Yom Kippur, which begins just after sunset, when you've eaten the meal that has to last you twenty-five hours and you feel full, ready and open, starts with an Aramaic prayer set to a famously beautiful melody. Kol Nidre, made famous beyond Jewish communitities by Max Bruch's setting for cello as recorded by Jacqueline du Pré, means 'All vows'. The short text asks that all the unfulfilled vows, oaths and consecrations that the individual has made to/with God during the previous year (or will make during the following year, depending on which liturgy you follow) be cancelled. To me, this seemed less like a prayer than a legal indemnification, like the terms and conditions we all scroll through before clicking 'agree' unthinkingly. Seth L. Sanders, the liberation philologist, says that Kol Nidre has been considered in that way by many Jewish scholars across a millennium, who have seen it as an embarrassment of transactional thinking. He calls modern iterations of this an 'oddly anti-Jewish-sounding criticism that the Kol Nidre formula is a mere set of empty technical formulas, echoing Paul's old attack [in 2 Corinthians] that "the letter of the law kills but the spirit gives life".'

Away from this self-shaming Ashkenazi rabbinical tradition, Sanders finds another interpretation in Jewish magic, something that was also not part of my school curriculum or conversations around the dinner table. In part, that's because this tradition comes from Babylonian Jews two millennia ago, and is therefore part of the history of Mizrahi Judaism, the multi-millennial communities of Jews who remained in Babylon after being exiled there in 586 BCE, subsequently migrating across South-West Asia and North Africa, with smaller communities settling in Central and East Asia. Mizrahi culture was completely hidden from me by Ashkenazi EW white supremacy.

Babylonian Jews were part of a lively community that included Christians, Mandaeans, Manicheans, Zoroastrians, pagans and, after the eighth century CE, Muslims.

All of them made magic bowls, and most of them used Babylonian Aramaic to write the inscriptions, because it was the language tradition in which the bowls were first made. Over time, Aramaic seems to have accrued the status of a code or spell, like Latin in medieval Europe: something half-understood, used for its deep association with old ways yet still lively and part of a living community. The incantation is generally written in an inward spiral, often with a female figure etched small at the centre, possibly referencing Lilith, Adam's first wife, who was associated with the demonic, and thus with cursing. The bowls were seen as having a protective function, which may derive from the relation of invocation to libation. Sanders quotes a Jewish incantation bowl that reads, 'Overturned are all vows [kol nidre] and curses and spells and magic and curses and magic and evil blows that may lodge in this man'. The physicality of 'overturned' suggests an outpouring of liquid as of the voice in prayer; both liquid and voice might trace the incised lettering, filling and being filled with the words' meaning, before spilling.

This is not rational, legalistic oath-breaking, but Sanders argues that the oaths overturned by Kol Nidre never were rational, legalistic transactions. He roots them in the demonic oaths treated by Babylonian spiritual-medical culture, quoting a prescription to cure 'the upper abdomen of a man [when it] hurts him as if the Oath bound him'. This sounds like the deep knots by which the body kips the pur: the silencing guilt, shame and anxiety that keep our solar plexuses verklempt. Kol Nidre is, in Sanders's liberatory reading, an unwinding of our own inner prohibitions; of the ways we have, having internalised dominance's fear-shaming, held ourselves back from speaking out, from naming ourselves, from gathering together in words, song and body language. In the beauty of the music and the rhythmic, rhyming repetitions, we pour ourselves into a very old ritual. According to magic bowls scholar Cyrus Gordon, Kol Nidre's 'purpose is to give the community a fresh start by annulling the evil forces set in motion by destructive (if unpremeditated) words'. To do so, we have to name those words and take responsibility for them.

Standing by your own word requires not only intention but attention. Dependent on context, every curse is also a cure – a pharmakon, a Greek word that means a medicine or poison derived from a herb or root, a tricky term made trickier by Jacques Derrida. In 'Plato's Pharmacy', as translated by Barbara Johnson, Derrida suggests that writing is a pharmakon, in the sense that it is 'a means of producing something', an effect that could help or harm; for him, the indeterminacy is the point. But pharmakon could be said to mean something like effectiveness, with its effects less dependent on indeterminacy than on attention. The range of effects of a plant extract depend on the plural possibilities within the plant, which plants themselves can alter these in attentive response to environmental stimuli. In preparation, effects depend on the attention and intent of the person doing the extraction. A nettle can sting; nettle stings can recalibrate histamine responses; and nettle tea can flush out toxins. It all depends on your knowledge and approach. We learn plant properties by season and climate, decide the preparation and measure the dosage by knowing the patient, and take responsibility for the results; the same is true for language.

Intent and attention come from the same root as tender: the Latin verb teneo, with its many contradictory meanings – or meanings that indicate our contradictory experiences – around holding and binding, from embracing to imprisoning. If we are not held soundly when we are babies, we may fight all later intent and attention, because any tenderness comes too close; any rest is experienced as arrest. To hold or be held can feel like being bound, which can feel like being cursed. Cursing, swearing and oathing all depend on the binding power of language: we can be contained by them, held down by dominance. Or we can find the cure in the curse, and think through the practical magic that is to hold yourself to something. There is a profound accountability in which, rather than referring upwards to authority, mutual (s)aid gives us strength because our being and our meaning are twined together, through both intention and tension.

Teneo is related to tanidan, the Persian verb for weaving, spinning and twisting. It carries an archaic sense of paying attention, as one would pay out thread. Here we are again in the grasp of textile-making. Our ambivalence about that tense power of attention and intention, of holding and being held, can be seen in the classical image of the Fates, who spin, measure and cut our lives. My great-grandmother was, in her Proust-reading days, a tapissière, a tapestry-artist who could sew or embroider anything. In her time as a registered alien in London during WWII, this included perfect copies of Chanel suits. She would try them on in department stores and snip out the labels to stitch into the versions she would then make from memory, adjusted for her height and (what she would call) embonpoint. What worked for her as self-fashioning fell flat when applied to me: I hated both her attempts to measure me for clothes I did not want – the final straw being a tutu – while telling me I was fat; and her attempts to teach me to sew, embroider, knit and crochet while telling me I had fat fingers. Getting glasses did not help: wound about with shame, my refusal had set in, as had her disdain. That we failed (to hear) each other remains a tender place in me, that I lost both the practical knowledge and the yarns I might have heard while learning with her.

Here is a tale that I could have heard my from great-grandmother, and that she could have heard from Reb Tsorke. We need to take a winding route to get there, because history is twisted. This tale is from the Pale of Settlement, which like the English Pale in Ireland was a colonial exclusion and detention zone. In this case, it was imposed by the Empress Catherine as part of her military expansion of Imperial Russia into the Ottoman Empire and Poland. Jews could not live in the cities of the Pale, and could not conduct business outside of its borders. The Pale's western border abutted Reb Tsorke's home province of Bukovina, an area that is now divided between Romania and Ukraine.

In my great-grandmother's childhood, Bukovina was the site of several devastating battles on the Eastern Front during WWI. With the dissolution of the Austro-Hungarian Empire, it initially joined the short-lived West Ukrainian National Republic, and then became part of the new independent nation of Romania mapped by the Versailles Treaty. Before her birth (in Bucharest, where her parents had relocated), Bukovina had been, in historical order, part of Kievan Rus; part of Hungary; the Principality of Moldavia; subject to Poland; independent of but occupied by Poland; a province of the Ottoman Empire for hundreds of years; occupied by the Russians; and gifted by the Russians at the Treaty of Küçük Kaynarca to the Habsburgs for their support against the Ottomans. It was at this moment that Catherine established the Pale to its east. A new border between Austro-Hungary and Russia became a line drawn across previously mobile and fluid Jewish communities.

The incantation bowls of Jewish Babylonia meet their equals in the bundle of curing and cursing practices found across the Ashkenazi diaspora, sometimes known dismissively as kishef, or women's magic. When they are documented, it is often through the sparse records of one place, with little way of tracing it to another. A custom documented in the Pale may or may not, given the mutability of borders and Bukovina, have crossed over to my maternal family. Knowledge transmission is partial, severed by the lies of Empire, migration, social mobility, patriarchy and the Sho'ah. So, even if I had yarned with my great-grandmother, I may never have heard of this custom, as she may not have done. I learned it, as I learned so many things, from a book. *For Times Such as These* by American feminist rabbis Ariana Katz and Jessica Rosenberg is a project of remaking Jewish tradition through feminist listending and mutual (s)aid. I followed an endnote to their book to a website, now dormant, which led me to an online article in *Vashti*, an independent British Jewish leftist feminist magazine. Wound into community, I take up responsibility for carrying this story in this baggy book.

Writing in *Vashti*, Annabel Gottfried Cohen, a Kohenet (priestess) who is reassembling women's spiritual traditions from the Pale, describes a ceremony called feldmestn – field measuring; in this particular case, cemetery measuring. The cemeteries were measured by groups of women who walked around them unspooling a long length of candle wick. It had been specifically spun and braided for this sacralising purpose, and would be subsequently cut to length for neshome likht (soul candles), also known as yahrzeit or memorial lights. These are large candles that burn for a full twenty-four hours, lit to mark the anniversary of a death. They are used collectively on Yom Kippur, a gateway day in which all of the Jewish living hover in waiting to see if we will be written into the Book of Life, with a protracted service of mourning and remembrance in the afternoon. It's impossible not to hear the echo of the Fates in this ceremony of spooling out the wick, then cutting it for the soul candles, then burning them, all on the boundary between the living and the dead.

The boundary measuring happened in preparation for Yom Kippur, during the late summer month of Elul, the last of the Jewish year, itself a boundary before the High Holy Days, a month marked by intense communal preparation and reflection. Counting out a community boundary measure within a state boundary, the women of the Pale were paid for this employment of maintaining the compass of cemeteries, beating the bounds of the living and the dead. There is nothing uncanny about this: the boundary was an economic definition useful both to local tax collectors and to synagogues that sold and maintained burial plots. In a busy month of preparing food and new clothes for the High Holy Days, feldmestn undoubtedly offered a chance to take a break from domestic responsibilities and walk in the falling soft late summer twilight, exchanging news, insights, gossip, tales, recipes, diagnoses, needs, new words – everything that spills and gets called spells, a word that is also rooted in spinning, that ancient mode of paying attention.

One way of describing the work of language is walking a boundary; as with the pharmakon, what matters and makes it matter is not indeterminacy, but our determination as to how we direct our attention. It is not about drawing a line as a closed border, but redefining the boundary itself as a place where things can happen.

In *Vashti*, Gottfried Cohen quotes from a tkhine, a prayer in Yiddish. This particular tkhine was contributed, anonymously, by an immigrant to the US, to a collection of tkhine published in New York in 1916. The prayer is titled 'Tkhine Ven Es Breykht Oys a Mageyfe'; a mageyfe is an epidemic, and the date of the publication uncannily foresees the coming post-war influenza pandemic. You can read and hear the whole prayer online, as I did, via the Open Siddur Project. Gottfried Cohen gives her own translation of the penultimate line, 'zol keyner nit feln in undzer gvul', as 'let no one be missing from our boundary'. Praying that a person or community comes back from the brink, that they do not cross over from the living to the dead, the tkhine resonates with the work of the feldmesterin as they walked that highly charged boundary.

There's a Yiddish word for doing the work where you are, not because where you are is special but because the work needs to be done: it's transliterated as doikayt or doykheit and many other versions besides, and it means hereness. Hereness arose of necessity from the frequent displacements by official decrees and other violence that shaped Ashkenazi experience. The Pale was not some essentialised, ahistorically 'Jewish' place, any more than the feldmesterin's work was essentialised women's work. Doikayt is what happens when the marginalised do the work because it's there to do, and do it where they are, in diaspora, because there is no other place in which to do it.

'Here where we live is our country': that was the principal principle of the Jewish Labour Bund (German word for union), active across Eastern Europe, a slogan that expanded doikayt into a manifesto for action. As leftist historian Molly Crabapple is charting in their ongoing project on the

Bund and doikayt (their transliteration of choice), organising means resisting borders and definitions. If we are seeds – diaspora means, at root, the scattering of seeds – then we grow where we land, in a theory and practice conceived in radical opposition to Zionism. The Pale was a place to learn (or it should have been) that states are a lie, names are a curse and hard borders are a garotte.

The Pale was a boundary place, but it was not a margin. While it was a place of oppression, it was also a place of irrepressible, improvisatory fluidity, of the liveliness that is summarised in doikayt. In *A Rainbow Thread*, his anthology on queer and trans Jewish history, Noam Sienna cites a letter to *Forverts*, the Yiddish-language newspaper in the US, written by Brooklynite Yeshaye Kotofsky, an immigrant from Krizover, in the Pale (now Kryve Ozero, formerly Krivoye Ozero, a nexus on trade routes across southern Ukraine and a thriving Jewish settlement in the early twentieth century). Kotofsky reports that a certain Berel went south from Krizover to see a professor in Odesa, and returned as 'a handsome, healthy, red-headed man'. Kotofsky was born in 1886, and he mentions Berel seeing a famous rabbi who died in 1883, so Berel's transition would have been narrated to him after the fact, but he was likely giving an eyewitness report of a man known to him personally. Under the name Berel-Beyle, incorporating his given name, this man gained a reputation as a mensch. He was welcomed into the prayer community at the synagogue from which he had previously been excluded in his assigned gender, and got married to an old girlfriend.

Let no one be missing from our boundary. That is the work of hereness. Here is the thing about boundaries: if we hold them open, they are mutable, pliable zones, not thin and rigid lines. A boundary is not a fixed border, and the feldmesterin knew that with their pacing bodies and spinning hands. A wick is not a line but a thickness. Not two-dimensional, but three. It has weight and width: if it did not, it could not absorb the fuel it needs to burn. The wick's dimension is reminiscent of adrienne maree brown's call in *Emergent Strategy* for an activist organising that is 'inch-wide and mile-deep', a hereness in opposition to the frantic, surface NGO model of mile-wide but inch-deep. A wick, like Le Guin's dragonhumans, carries within it the potential for fire, which is the potential for transformation. A gathering of threads that gathers us together, a wick holds within its inch width the fiery spark of the universe.

A conduit between this life and the next, a wick is what I twist, measure with, cut to length and light when writing from and about memory. Working in this boundary feels like lighting (myself as) a soul candle, a pharmakon of fire that both burns me down and lights my way. At the end of the long process, I burn with shame at the unresolved conundrum that Hanif Abdurraqib articulates in his *New Yorker* essay 'In Defense of Despair':

> Language fails at the feet of an empire's violence; language fails to scale the ever-growing wall between who is and isn't deemed worthy of a life. Yet I am trying to use this same failing machinery to communicate how, for the sake of my own fragile heart, and sometimes fragile brain, I remain more committed to honesty than I do to optimism.

It is only by using language that we can change it – and, through it, the world in which we speak.

This is something that Le Guin knew, in her familial bones. Le Guin's father was an anthropologist, Alfred Kroeber, who long before her birth as the youngest child of his second marriage, had both a complicated friendship and a professional relationship with a man who came to be called Ishi, although that was not his name. Ishi means man in Yahi, an Indigenous language of which he was one of the last speakers. He did not have a name because Yahi social protocols required that another speaker give your name when introducing you to strangers. But he arrived alone, and was given the name by those who took him in, or took him over, at the museum of anthropology in San Francisco, where he subsequently met Kroeber, who had founded the department of anthropology at the University of California at Berkeley, across the bay.

In her essay 'Indian Uncles', Le Guin reflects on how little she knew about Ishi, because her father responded to his death from tuberculosis with 'the muteness of undesired complicity and the dumbness of the bereaved'. Kroeber's complicity arose because he was on the other side of the country when Ishi died, and could not prevent the violation of an autopsy that led to a 'grotesque division of the body', in Le Guin's words. The forensic word for such a violation is disarticulation, a striking recognition of the connection between the body and self-expression, and of the violence that destroys both.

When the University of California Press sought, in the slowly changing atmosphere of the 1950s, to commission a book that recognised Ishi as a person rather than an object, they asked Kroeber, but he declined. Le Guin writes:

neither he nor his science had a vocabulary for his knowledge. And if he couldn't find the right words, he wouldn't use the wrong ones.

> Not long after Ishi's death, my father took leave
> from anthropology, was psychoanalyzed, and practiced
> analysis for some years. But I don't think Freud had
> quite the words he needed, either.

Le Guin's mother, Theodora Kroeber, who had married Alfred nine years after Ishi's death, would take up the commission, writing two books about Ishi; two of Le Guin's brothers, Karl and Clifton Kroeber, would write a third book, *Ishi in Three Centuries*, which includes chapters on repatriation, responsibility and writing against genocide.

Le Guin herself wrote her fiction, poetry and essays from the tensions of a thoughtful childhood spent around both academic anthropologists and Indigenous people, two of whom she recalls in 'Indian Uncles': 'the Papago Juan Dolores and the Yurok Robert Spott'. In the final sentences of her essay, she notes of her child self: 'I didn't know anything. I thought everybody spoke Yurok. But I knew where the center of the world was' – in watching her 'father and Robert, one listening, the other telling'. Listending differently centres her work: Ged, the titular wizard of Earthsea, is described as having coppery skin, a fact that cover artists largely and determinedly ignored, subsequent to Ruth Robbins, who created a striking woodcut with reddish skin tones for the original edition. In essay after essay, and story after story, Le Guin attended to the myth of manifest destiny and the people and places it violated, and to the tensions in her own privileged relation to that myth. Few white American writers have (and perhaps could have) written, as she wrote in 'A Non-Euclidean View of California as a Cold Place to Be', first published in the *Yale Review* in December 1983: 'the words "holocaust" and "genocide" are fashionable now; but not often are they applied to American history. We were not told in school in Berkeley that the history of California had the final solution for its first chapter.'

In her tribute to Le Guin for *Kenyon Review*, Chumash/ Esselen poet Deborah A. Miranda generously observed and gathered the 'quieter tweets, Facebook posts, and of course, private emails, from all the "invisibles" whom Ursula had befriended and championed', which poured out after Le Guin's death in January 2018. Miranda tells the story of a writing workshop she participated in, following which Le Guin made a beeline to thank her for the poem she had read:

> A friend said to me, 'You know who her father was, don't you?' I shook my head. My friend told me. It was a name of an anthropologist who had done a lifetime of work with California Indians; who had, in fact, been a key player in declaring the Esselen tribe – my tribe – extinct.
>
> The daughter of that man had just acknowledged a poem by the daughter of an Indigenous man from the Esselen Nation, a poem about still existing eighty years later, despite that academic denial. Ursula did not have to acknowledge me. She certainly did not have to compliment my work. But that was Ursula.

Le Guin says in 'Indian Uncles' that from Spott she learned:

> a very Yurok moral sentiment, shame. Not guilt, there was nothing to be guilty about; just shame. You blush resentfully, you hold your tongue, and you figure it out. I have Robert to thank in part for my deep respect for shame as a social instrument. Guilt I believe to be counterproductive, but shame can be immensely useful; if, for

example, any member of Congress was acquainted in any form with shame – well, never mind.

She minded; she attended. Shame is not the fear of loss of status it first provokes. If we can get beyond fear, shame is an ethical attention to being in relation, listening to the world around you. It was that listening that gave her the steps she used intentionally, attentively, throughout her long career, to change her mind: you hear the critique and feel it; you take a breath and a moment of silence; you become aware of the fear of status loss, and let it go. In that difficult freedom, you figure out what you did, and how to do differently, ethically, through the teaching set before you.

The word shame is another of those powerful words whose roots are obscured, but the reliably prissy *OED* says that 'many scholars assume a pre-Germanic *skem-, variant of *kem- to cover ... "covering oneself" being the natural expression of shame'. Natural is doing a lot of work in that claim. Freud similarly claimed that plaiting and weaving are the only technologies invented by women, who did so imitatively based on the growth of pubic hair 'that conceals the genitals', and in order to cover them further. Shame, covering: what a scam. In Le Guin's hands, rather than a cover-up, shame is something that uncovers and demands further uncovering.

The heat of it. As if you were transforming into a dragon, fire held within your cheeks. To breathe fire is an ambiguous feeling: it can be an unbearable intensification, but it can also be a release. The breath that I was taught with which to unwind my solar plexus is described as a deep, slow inhalation followed by a purse-lipped exhalation – like slowly blowing out a candle. It is not easy. If you are someone who holds a lot of knotted tension in your solar plexus, releasing it can feel like being punched, like wanting to throw up and to eat everything you shouldn't at the same time, like wanting to cry and moan, like wanting to never feel anything like this again. All the covering up, the self-silencing, following the order of service, the Oath that binds us, has to be felt in order to let it go. And oh, it hurts. We all carry this burning dragon inside us, and it is as much work to hold it in as it is to hold space for letting it go.

I want to call this trans-piration: this breath, this unwinding, these language acts that emerge from letting go, and in turn feel like it. A breathing-across-together. Transpiration originates in alchemy, where it meant vapours emitted through a porous surface: a parallel for how language emerges from inside of us. To cis-spire, to hoard our breath or meaning inside in one fixed place, out of fear of ourselves or each other, is to ex-pire. Transpire has come to mean to happen or occur, a misuse that gives the *OED*itors a fit of the vapours, but that's what language does: it makes happen happen, and in doing so makes other things happen.

We make ourselves up by going through the cur(s)e: the burning sense that we have been had, that we have been bound, that the Oath has knotted our vitals and we have lived with it rather than shame ourselves by speaking our pain, asking for help and being responsible for the cure. Most of us have access to few shared ceremonies under dominance culture, because it seeks to erase them. We need them: precise, incised, full of intent and attention. Fighting with the dictionary, word by word, is my incantation bowl to break the demonic Oath of dominance. If we attend to the gaps and fissures that arise when words are said to have (as so many of us do) plural and undocumented origins, there we can make our own meanings, by listening intently, intimately, curiously, associatively.

And we need to, because language is, like breath, water and food, one of the blazing and necessary ways in which we ingest and interact with our worlds. We can use it – or let it be used on us – to destroy those connections, or we can participate in weaving them. We are mired in language that erects the 'ever-growing wall between who is and isn't deemed worthy of a life', as Abdurraqib writes. It is easy to succumb to that, to let anti-semic dominance knot us and disembody us so there is neither hearing nor here-ing. Doykait means feeling our weight: the weight of our words is our weight on the world, our way of carrying the weight of the world. Up against the ever-growing wall, it is hard to hold onto the thread of making ourselves and each other up, to find words that can heal in the face of words that hurt.

Yet admitting that words and names *can* hurt us is the start, the beginning that is a cut and the cry from it. The shame that burns when we do this. And from that, the deep breath, the reflection, the next step, the next many steps, taken messily together. There is no easy win, no one simple life hack, no one-size-fits-all, no once-and-for-all victory over dominance – not because dominance is strong, but because it shamelessly steals from us. I was frequently told off as a child for 'having to have the last word'. That meant *my* word, my right to speak, my desperate protest asserting my right to exist in the face of my father's assumed right to all the words, and particularly the final word, end of. It is hard to end this when I still do not know the magic word that can keep us all safe. In the writing of this book, over and over, for three years or nine years or my entire writing life, since the Pyrrhic victory of the felt pens that felt like ashes in my mouth, I have been learning what I will be going to have realised when I let go of this manuscript, this chapter, this sentence: that the magic word is all of them, continuing.

We keep weaving our baggy text/iles to hold the wild oats that keep us going while we take a stand, or a knee, at our protests for freedom of association, carrying our signs that, in their compact compasses, bear mile-deep histories of witness. Aflame with fear-shame, we remain attentive, accountable; allowed, in our ceremony of belief, to restart.

If we are to go through the curse that is bad language, we must, over and over and over, fill and spill the bowl whose incantation breaks the fear-shame that binds us. For our words and gestures to be the thread we twist to mark a people-place – haciendo caras, making soul (candles) – we must let no one be missing from our boundary. We are our only book of life. We are here, gathered together, in this list-ending. As we take a breath together to light this candle, what will we uncover as we spill?

SOURCES

Are you feeling sourcey? Writing a book is sorcery that mixes a libation from many sources to make its incantation.

EW non-fiction writing gives primacy to the written word as its evidentiary paradigm, and I have followed this throughout, giving the authors and titles of books and articles within the text, in such a way as I hope you can follow the thread for yourselves. For me, this is a feminist practice of citation, as theorised by Clare Hemmings and Sara Ahmed (and, more informally, by Rebecca Colesworthy *@rcolesworthy* on Bluesky, who suggested that citation can be a summoning spell). In this section, I mix written texts into my incantation bowl with other evidentiary paradigms, such as conversations for which there are no traces or transcripts.

This book began in an online conversation: struggling back on an intercity train from a freelance gig in early 2016, I asked friends on Facebook whether I should start a TinyLetter of fortnightly opinions about cinema, life and everything. They said yes. As detailed in chapter 4, I was thinking towards the publication of my essay in *Not That Bad: Dispatches from Rape Culture*, edited by Roxane Gay. Over two years, I wrote twenty-six letters from A to Z, and had maybe as many as twenty-six responsive readers. Particular thanks to regular reader, friend and interlocutor Theo Chiotis, who said very early: 'These letters should be a book.' This is not that book, and it is. Iykyk.

Behind every word in the book that this is (and the many that it isn't), there is a conversation with Sam Fisher, my editor, colleague, co-conspirator and friend. Le Guin, when asked by the *TLS,* 'If you could make a change to anything you've written over the years, what would it be?', replied:

In *The Dispossessed*, I would mention the communal
pickle barrels at street corners in the big towns,
restocked by whoever in the community has made or
kept more pickles than they need. I knew about the free
pickles all along, but never could fit them into the book.

Sam, you're the pickle barrel: you fed this book, gave it salt
and bite, and you preserved its existence when I flailed.

The biggest thanks also to the Peninsula editorial team
of Jake Franklin and Will Rees, to copy editor extraordi-
naire Odhran O'Donoghue, illuminating cover artist David
Pearson and canny PR Liam Konemann. It takes a shtetl to
make a book, oy.

If this book flows, it is because of all the teas, coffees and
other beverages I've been gifted during its writing, including
a life-saving iced coffee with Will Forrester when the flailing
became serious. Alison Croggon's *Monsters*, both the book
and its writing process, is a deep intertext here, and one day
we will get that flat white (Melbourne-style) in person again.
I think of cardamom coffee and fennel tea with Tobias Wray
and Masha Vlasova giving life at Arteles artists' residency in
Finland; herbal teas by the sea with Elhum Shakerifar, talking
translation and hums; the best hot (& cold) chocolates with
Jack Thompson (& Sid), thinking about queer and trans lit;
cold CBD cans in the park with Rebekah Polding, gemæcce
and close reader; roasted barley tea, picture books and Cecilia
Vicuña stories with Hyun Jin Cho, Laurence Byrne and
Namu; cold brew oolong with Chi Ta-Wei (with thanks to
Yi Wang), which made the final climate-change-broiled draft
possible. Drafts and draughts are needed when things get hot.
SF Said and Jenny Chamarette brewed me pints of courage
when I was panicking, with their perceptive and prophetic

comments on the penultimate draft. Tom de Ville exchanged manuscripts with me, and we swam rather than drank Pells Pool as we thought about horrors and ancestors.

Sometimes a recorded conversation can make you feel a part of it: David Naimon's extraordinary podcast *Between the Covers* plays in the background of this book, particularly episodes with Dionne Brand, adrienne maree brown, Vajra Chandrasekera, Hélène Cixous, Álvaro Enrigue, Bhanu Kapil, Nam Le, Canisia Lubrin, Adania Shibli and Cecilia Vicuña. I took a poetry workshop with Cecilia at Naropa during a season of forest fires, and witnessed her words bringing rain: a few drops, but enough. The work I did in her class untangled and rebraided me, as a writer and a person. Her work is always a revelation.

My deep conversation with Le Guin begins in childhood, but would never have restarted without the startle of teaching the *Earthsea* series as a TA for Daniel Heath Justice in 2005–06. Daniel's wisdom has kept me company for two decades, through our Miss Kitties' conversations about world-building, writing and rewriting, especially an exchange of my preface and his introduction for the twentieth-anniversary edition of his path-clearing book *Our Fire Survives the Storm: A Cherokee Literary History, Citizenship and Sovereignty Edition*. He made this a better book by encouraging me to listend for hope where I heard despair.

Working on Le Guin's words for *Space Crone* and *The Word for World* with Sarah Shin has opened my eyes, over and over, to the power of oneiric feminism and its dragonfire, and brought me into many conversations about Le Guin, language and power with Sarah, and with Theo Downes-Le Guin, Bhanu Kapil, Kelly Link, Una McCormack, David Naimon, Julie Phillips, Nisha Ramayya and SF Said, all of whose wider and wiser wordworks resonate across this book.

It's the honour of my life to work with English PEN as co-chair of the Translation Advisory Group, and to be a very small part of a transnational, transhistorical, urgent conversation about freedom and equity of expression. This book resonates with and through ongoing conversations with colleagues there including Sim Eldem, Will Forrester, Dan Gorman, Cat Lucas and Nadia Saeed.

Inhale

This quotation from Nam Le came up as part of an online discussion of Nam's appearance on on David Naimon's podcast *Between the Covers* to talk about his book *36 Ways of Writing a Vietnamese Poem*, released on 17 March 2024. Thanks to Odhran O'Donohue for locating the source in Nam's essay 'David Malouf's new words', *The Monthly*, April 2019.

Ray Borg and I have had a number of conversations about queer BDSM, religion and repression since Folkestone & Hythe Council banned a screening of Ray's film *Passion* at Folkestone Documentary Festival in 2022.

'We cannot resign ... but we can re-sign' was a pun that arose in conversation on Twitter with poet Khairani Barokka, around our resignations from the Society of Authors in 2023, over the SoA's refusal to speak out against, or even name, the genocide in Gaza.

Gloria Anzaldúa committed to publishing with feminist small presses such as Kitchen Table and Aunt Lute. This makes her books difficult to find in the UK (they were difficult to keep in stock even when I worked at the Toronto Women's Bookstore two decades ago), but very much worth it.

Ambi- was written umbe or ymbe in medieval English, and was widely used as a prefix for verbs that mean to go, hold, dig around; umbebraid, vmbeclyppe, umbefold, umbe-lap, umbelouk, umbethink, umbeweave could be revived to help us think in and of our surroundings.

With thanks to poet and lapsed Catholic Tracy Ryan, who long ago gave me feminist permission to carry out an exor-cism. If all you have to hand is a bicycle bell, some market-stall nag champa and the poems of Catullus, use them. They work.

Ancestors is the third book in adrienne maree brown's Grievers trilogy (published by AK Press), and it arrived like a blessing as I was finishing this book.

Most of the trans, queer and feminist Jewish scholars and activists cited herein are American. Shout-out to the UK's Queer Yeshiva, and to writers Amy Acre, Anna Coatman, Ray Filar and Sam Solomon for thinking through with me what it means to be a queer feminist anti-Zionist Jewish writer here. Shout-outs too to Sarah Crewe and Peter Scalpello for comparative religious thinking on these questions.

In 'Composition as explanation', first delivered in Cambridge in 1925 and published by the Hogarth Press, Gertrude Stein said, 'Continuous present is one thing and beginning again and again is another thing. These are both things.' This book tries to do both.

Beginning

Ted Chamberlin taught me comparative literature in grad-uate school, where he first prompted me to think about why we can lie. He also introduced me to the Sapir–Whorf hypothesis, which appears in chapter 5, but only I am to blame for the related puns.

I encountered Seth L. Sanders's work via Bluesky, where he is *@nabalkattu*. I hate and I love social media, as I hate and I love myself. It is the One Ring we bear. Like the One Ring, it has helped me build fellowship with which to travel through dark times, but it has also left deep scars. Blog posts are available on Sanders's website at sethlsanders.wordpress.com.

I use 'every tool is a weapon if you hold it right' as a proverb, but I'm startled to remember that it is, in fact, a song lyric by Ani Difranco ('My IQ').

Bi+ Lines is a poetry project by Helen Bowell, with an anthology published by fourteen poems, and it's where I encountered bi+ as a sexily inclusive notation for two or more.

On vaybertaytsh, see Rokhl Kafrissen, 'Queer Yiddishkeit', *The Tablet*, 19 June 2019.

On Lies, Secrets, and Silence is the title of Adrienne Rich's selected prose, 1966–78, a book that deeply impressed me as a young feminist poet. Rich was instrumental in the writing and publication of Janice Raymond's *The Transsexual Empire*, a hateful manual for transphobes.

STC's phrase comes from *Biographia Literaria*, in which he associates it with 'poetic faith': a lot to unpack there about religion and the arts as magic.

@martinrue mentioned Tucuya on #langsky, and generously shared with me Janet Barnes's paper 'Evidentials in the Tucyua verb', *International Journal of American Linguistics* (50.3, 1984). The *Economist* article I discuss is paywalled.

Brockington et al, 'Storytelling increases oxytocin and positive emotions and decreases cortisol and pain in hospitalized children', *PNAS* (118.22, 2021).

I bought Sara Ahmed's *Living a Feminist Life* at Gay's the Word as a Valentine's Day gift to myself in 2017, and have a pellucid memory of 'feminist snap' while reading it later that night, stunned and stirred, in a guest room at Stirling University. Her reading of 'The Willful Child' made it possible for me to write 'trigger', the twenty-first newsletter, where I finally delineated the sexual abuse.

Elhum Shakerifar drew my attention to the enfolded quotation from John Berger in Naomi Klein's *Doppelganger* when we were talking about relaxation-based anxiety.

We call these trips Freudian slips because Siggi named them. He coined Fehlleistungen, which literally means mis-performances or failures to achieve, in *The Psychopathology of Everyday Life*. James Strachey then coined parapraxis for his translation, Vol. VI, Hogarth Press Standard Edition.

Anatoly Liberman (book-man) is an outstanding example of nominative determinism, which we'll meet in chapter 2. His post on Grimm's etymology, 'The multifaceted art of lying', was published on *OUPblog* on 15 August 2018.

Caroline Darian wrote a powerful book, *I'll Never Call Him Dad Again: Turning Our Family Trauma of Chemical Submission into a Collective Fight*, translated by Stephen Brown. The original French title is better: *Et j'ai cessé de t'appeler papa*, which I would translate as *And I Stopped Calling You Dad*. Stopping is necessary for a restart.

The grainy roots of legere came via Rajni Shah's *Experiments in Listening*, in which they quote Gemma Corradi Fiumara's *The Other Side of Language: A Philosophy of Listening* quoting Martin Heidegger's *Early Greek Thinking*, translated by David Farrell Krell and Frank A. Capuzzi, on legein relating to gathering crops. Shah notes that they feel 'simultaneously resolved and ambivalent' to be quoting a Nazi philosopher.

Palabrarmas is excerpted in Suzanne Jill Levine and Eliot Weinberger's English translation and selection of Vicuña's work, *Unravelling Words & the Weaving of Water*. Book Works made her first book, *Saborami*, originally published in the UK in a handmade limited edition, available again in 2024.

In 2022, the BBC's nationwide study of 7,000 NHS dental practices found that nine in ten were not taking on new adult NHS patients, and eight in ten were not taking on children. Fuck the Tories.

Naming

I gave my nibling a pencil and notebook set after they told me: 'I want to be an aufor but not like you, Auntie So, a real one with my books in *shops*.'

I read Dylan Robinson's *Hungry Listening: Resonant Theory for Indigenous Sound Studies* while putting together the first draft of this book in 2022, and its resonance remains.

Gabriel Bodard intoned 'nomen est omen' to me during an artist residency at the Institute of Classical Studies, University of London, in summer 2023, which made this book possible. The Plutarch snark is all my own.

Noah Berlatsky offers a useful summary in 'Censoring Anne Frank's diary because of "sexuality" is not just denigrating but a smokescreen', *Independent*, 21 Septermber 2023. Fuck fascists.

Gay's the Word have ACT UP NY's Silence=Death watermelon badges.

The NHS document on ODD is from Essex Partnership University NHS Foundation Trust, with the Lighthouse Child Development Centre. Rupinder K Legha says it all: 'There are no bad kids: an antiracist approach to oppositional defiant disorder', *Pediatrics* (155.2, 2025).

Steve McQueen's film *Hunger* (2008) is I think the first and only British or Irish feature film about the hunger strikes and dirty protests. So much radical UK and Irish history is missing from our screens and shelves.

Interpellation comes from LA's 1970 essay for *La Pensée*, 'Ideology and ideological state apparatuses (notes towards an investigation)', translated into English by Ben Brewster.

I read *On Tyranny* as a graphic novel illustrated by Nora Krug.

Yásnaya Elena Aguilar Gil's manifesto 'Ää Ayuujk Jëntiky Nääjxwi'nyët' or 'Languages and nation-states' formed the basis for *Funambulist* 53: Thread of Translations (April 2024), where it was translated from Ayuujk into thirty non-hegemonic languages.

Roland Barthes, *S/Z: An Essay*, translated by Richard Mille, and published in 1970.

The Lancet reported on 10 January 2025 that the true death toll from Gaza is at least 41 per cent higher than reported figures, in Zeina Jamaluddine et al., 'Traumatic injury mortality in the Gaza Strip from Oct 7, 2023, to June 30, 2024: a capture–recapture analysis' (405.10477). Yaakov Garb's report for *Harvard Dataverse*, published in June 2025, demonstrated that almost 400,000 people have disappeared from Gaza's pre-genocide population of 2.2 million. Fuck Israel and its supporters.

Zadie Smith's essay was published on 5 May 2024 in *The New Yorker*. Thank you to Will Forrester for an important conversation about this essay and its implications (and a cold yuzu tea). Isabella Hammad's essay was published on 13 June 2024 in the *New York Review of Books*. Andrea Long Chu's essay 'The free speech debate is a trap' was published on 22 December 2023 in *New York* magazine. All three are paywalled.

The Electronic Intifada's tribute 'In memory of Dr Refaat Alareer' was published on 7 December 2023, and includes excerpts from the live conversation. We Are Not Numbers co-founders Ahmed Alnaouq and Pam Bailey edited a collection of work by their participants, *We Are Not Numbers: The Voices of Gaza's Youth*. Always carry a marker.

David Graeber's *Direct Action: An Ethnography* was published by AK Press in 2009, and has only become more relevant since.

Sara Ahmed's phrases appear in 'Feminist Killjoys (and other willful subjects)', *The Scholar and Feminist Online* (8.3, 2010); 'Sexism: the problem with a name', *new formations* (86, 2015); and 'Letter from a Feminist Killjoy' on Ahmed's blog, dated 27 November 2024.

I couldn't have written this book without online community projects like the Nonbinary Hebrew Project, World Atlas of Language Structures, Open Siddur Project, archive. org, and Wikipedia.

The feminist Ashamnu and Al Chet prayers by Abby Citrin, Rabbi Danya Ruttenberg, Emily Becker, Guila Benchimol, Leah Greenblum, S. Bear Bergman and Shira Berkovits were published in *The Forward*, 7 Septermber 2018.

'The body kips the pur' is an homage to Bessel Van Der Kolk's book, *The Body Keeps the Score*.

Calling

Kristin Hersh tells this story in her memoir *Paradoxical Undressing*, called *Rat Girl* in the US. Naomi Klein's first book *No Logo* discusses how alternative third-wave feminisms got mainstreamed into commercialised confessionalism.

I first read Anne Carson's 'The gender of sound' in 1998, in her American collection *Glass, Irony & God*. It's finally available in the UK as a Silver Press Portals pocket essay, thirty years after its original publication.

My notes on Freud here emerge from discussions with my queer feminist therapist, Leah Davidson, as well as from Elisabeth Bronfen's *The Knotted Subject: Hysteria and its Discontents*, Joseph Schwartz's *Cassandra's Daughter: A History of Psychoanalysis* and Jeffrey Moussaieff Masson's *The Assault on Truth*.

In *Landscape, Gender and Ritual Space: The Ancient Greek Experience*, Susen Guettel Cole reads Hippocratic accounts through Artemisian rituals, including the haunting one of hanging dolls in trees, which is preferable to forced marriage.

I've learned about breathing, speaking and the solar plexus through practices facilitated by dancer and visual artist Sharone Halevy, somatics facilitator and activist Kat Hobbs, and singer and historian CN Lester.

In her essay 'Myth and Archetype in Science Fiction' (1976), published in *The Language of the Night*, Le Guin writes that, 'we all have the same kind of dragons in our psyche, just as we all have the same kind of heart and lungs in our body'. Thanks to Sarah Shin for this quotation.

Nisha Ramayya's book *States of the Body Produced by Love* offers crucial thoughts on the imperial projects of PIE and Monier Monier-Williams' Sanskrit dictionary.

I learned about the sensory homunculus in Gwyneth Jones's speculative fiction novel *Band of Gypsys*, one of many reasons to read her *Bold as Love* series.

Theorising what I'm calling gut instinct here, Antonio Damasio writes in *Feeling & Knowing* that 'feelings provide the mind with facts on the basis of which we know effortlessly that whatever else is in mind at the moment also belongs to us, is happening to us'. Fuck Descartes.

Noreen Masud pointed me to Klein's use of pipik after I tweeted something about Yiddish. Noreen's book *A Flat Place* gave me a way to think about traversing my body and memory as a landscape.

Toni Morrison's keynote 'A humanist view' was delivered on 30 May 1975, at Portland State University's Center for Black Studies, and republished online on 26 March 2025 by *The Black Agenda Review*.

Morrison's reader's report on Davis's *An Autobiography* was published online by Columbia Rare Books & Manuscript Library on 18 January 2022.

M. Gessen's 'The Putin Paradigm' appeared on 13 December 2016 in the *New York Review of Books*. It's paywalled.

Alaa Abd el-Fattah's 2017 article 'A portrait of the activist outside his prison' is included in *You Have Not Yet Been Defeated: Selected Works 2011–2021*, translated by a collective and introduced by Naomi Klein. Alaa is currently still illegally detained, and his mother, Laila Soueif, is hospitalised on hunger strike.

Marwan Kaabour's *The Queer Arab Glossary* is why I wanted to give this book a glossary of coinages for a long time, but I knew it couldn't be as sexy or collective as his, so there's this bibliographic essay instead.

I came upon *How to Kill a Dragon* randomly while browsing the philology shelves at the Institute of Classical Studies library. My favourite bit is where Watkins quotes Sappho 1 and notes that it throws off his whole analysis, but has no way to read its topping from the bottom wordplay.

Butler's *Parting Ways* has only become more painfully relevant since its publication. That is what prophecy does, as we'll see in chapter 4.

Crying

Anne Carson includes Euripides' *Orestes* in place of *Eumenides* in her *An Oresteia*.

I looked up blasphemy (as I did historia) in *The Cambridge Greek Lexicon*, the first new Greek-English dictionary in about a century, notable for correctly translating sexual terms. The nineteenth-century Greek-English dictionary translated the verb laikazo as to wench, but *CGL* gives the correct definition of perform fellatio. I call it the sucking-dictionary.

Rabbi Danya Ruttenberg's 'the desert speaks' was published on 8 February 2024 in her *Life is a Sacred Text* newsletter, hosted on Ghost. Fuck Substack.

Carson translated *Agamemnon* in *An Oresteia*, where Kassandra's speech is translated at one point as '[screams] [screams] [screams]'. In the introduction, Carson writes that she 'spent years trying to grasp Kassandra in words'.

J. L. Austin defined performative language in *How to Do Things With Words*, a title I envy.

The seventh line of Rainer Maria Rilke's *Duino Elegies*, 'Ein jeder Engel ist schrecklich', is often translated as 'every angel is terrifying'. Schreck can mean scare, start or shock, so it could equally be 'every angel is a start(le)'.

'Testimonial injustice' came via Chanda Prescod-Weinstein *@chanda* on Bluesky. It was coined by Miranda Fricker in *Epistemic Injustice: Power and the Ethics of Knowing*.

Peter T. Leeson and Jacob W. Russ, 'Witch trials', *The Economic Journal* (128, 2017), is considered an authoritative source on the numbers.

Joanna Bourke's thorough study *Rape: A History from 1860 to the Present* is a useful place to begin to understand EW legal and cultural frameworks.

Maryse Condé should have won the Nobel Prize for Literature.

No/Thing

I don't know what I make of Bloom's argument that J was a (wealthy, privileged) woman, but his reading certainly startled me productively when I found it on the shelf at the bookstore where I worked when I was nineteen.

Discussing Indo-Iranian formulaic phrases, Watkins cites Kurke's article 'Pouring prayers: a formula of IE sacral poetry?' in the Journal of Indo-European Studies (17, 1989), noting that she highlights the projected IE word *gheu-, pouring – which is also the ultimate referent for the OED's connection of God to libation.

'No ideas but in things' is from Book 1 of William Carlos Williams's poem Paterson.

Damasio's *Feeling and & Knowing* pointed me to Roger Penrose's *The Emperor's New Mind*.

This is my first and only citation of the *Guardian*, which I try to avoid because of its institutionalised transphobia. Michael Rosen is a mensch.

You can download printable bust cards by UK region from the Green and Black Cross website, in the 'Guides, Resources and Other Organisations' section.

'Yes, and' comes from Keith Johnstone's life-enhancing book *Impro: Improvisation and the Theatre*.

Margaret Killjoy generously allowed Silver Press' blog to republish her 2007 interview with Le Guin, on 28 October 2024.

The 1824 Vagrancy Act will be repealed in 2026, after a campaign by university students. However, it will be replaced by new laws criminalising begging and trespassing. Fuck Labour.

Laleh Khalili quotes Marcus Rediker's observation on yarning in her book *The Corporeal Life of Seafaring*.

Ted Chiang's 'Story of Your Life' is published in *Stories of Your Life and Others*, and is much better than its film adaptation as *Arrival*. Samuel Delany's *Babel-17* deserves a chapter of its own for its linguistics-as-technology fireworks.

'Darmok' is all writers' favourite episode of *TNG*. SF Said introduced me to it, and to the Trekverse. The final two drafts of this book were deeply shaped by watching *Voyager*. You can find the text of Le Guin's *TV Guide* article on Tumblr and Reddit, but I first encountered it in David Seitz's book *A Different* Trek: *Radical Geographies of* Deep Space Nine.

The interview with Lilith Bardakçi by Sim Eldem is titled 'Lubunca is the language of activism', and was published on *PEN Transmissions* on 7 December 2023.

María Rosa Menocal's *Shards of Love: Exile and the Origin of the Lyric* is a lasting inspiration for writing about the potency of the vernacular, and how poets might unmake official language.

Christina Sharpe's *Ordinary Notes* is a compendium of attention and listending to the ways in which languages – verbal, visual, monumental – are the crusading companions of Empire.

Hortense Spillers, 'Mama's baby, papa's maybe: an American grammar book', *Diacritics* (17.2, 1987) is a foundational essay for Black feminist literary studies, and therefore for literary studies.

Anne Balsamo's book, in which she embeds cyberfeminism in personal and political histories, is *Technologies of the Gendered Body: Reading Cyborg Women*.

The Well of Loneliness by Radclyffe Hall is multiply famed for its bad language. It was tried for obscenity in 1928; on appeal, the judge described it as 'more subtle, demoralising, corrosive, corruptive, than anything that was ever written'. Jeanette Winterson, who acknowledged that the book helped her come out, described it as 'one of the worst books yet written'. Both badges of pride.

Saidiya Hartman defines the work of critical fabulation as 'impossible writing that attempts to say that which resists being said' in 'Venus in two acts' in *Small Axe* (12.2, 2008).

Rachel Pollack's *Seventy-Eight Degrees of Wisdom* has been in print continuously since 1980. It's often referred to as the 'Bible of Tarot', which is delightful blasphemy for a spiritual book by a trans Jew.

Courtney Alexander, adrienne maree brown, Charlie Claire Burgess, CAConrad, Frank Duffy, Elicia Epstein, Tayannah Lee McQuillar, Junauda Petrus, Oliver Pickle, Tillie Walden, Ruth West, and Nyasha Williams are contemporary Tarot thinkers and artists whose work informs my reading here.

Exhale

Mona Eltahawy published 'Why I say "fuck"' on her blog, *Feminist Giant*, on 18 December 2020.

The possible origin of curse comes from Anatoly Liberman's 'Blessing and cursing, part 3: curse (conclusion)', published on 2 November 2016 on the *OUPblog*.

Sanders's reading is in '"Lonely and Naked ... before the throne of God:" On the role of philology in understanding religious experience', published on his blog, 28 March 2025.

Jacques Derrida's essay was first published in his collection *Dissemination*.

Annabel Gottfried Cohen's 'The forgotten women's rituals of Yom Kippur' was published on *Vashti*, 25 Septermber 2020.

Molly Crabapple's *Here Where We Live is Our Country: The Story of the Jewish Labor Bund*, is forthcoming.

A Rainbow Thread: An Anthology of Queer Jewish Texts from the First Century to 1969 is edited by Noam Sienna with a kehillah of translators.

The information on Krizover comes from jewua.org, *History of Jewish Communities in Ukraine*, run by Ukrainian-Jewish software engineer Chaim (Vitaly) Burak.

Hanif Abdurraqib, 'In defence of despair', *The New Yorker*, 16 May 2025. It's paywalled.

Theodora Kroeber's books were *Ishi in Two Worlds: A Biography of the Last Wild Indian in North America*, published in 1961, and *Ishi, Last of His Tribe*, published in 1964 by Parnassus Press, who would soon after invite Le Guin to write a children's book for them – and *A Wizard of Earthsea* was born. Both Parnassus books were illustrated by Ruth Robbins.

Deborah A. Miranda's 'Ursula K. Le Guin has walked on' was published in *Kenyon Review*'s 'In Memoriam' online special collection.

Sadie Plant's *Zeros + Ones* introduced me both to Ada Lovelace and to Freud's wacky yet memorable ideas about textiles and shame.

*

Freud shouldn't get the final word, so here is a Le Guin thread.

The Carrier Bag Theory of Fiction is available as a pocket essay published by Ignota Press.

A Wizard of Earthsea, *The Tombs of Atuan*, *The Farthest Shore*, *Tehanu*, *Tales from Earthsea* (including 'Dragonfly') and *The Other Wind* are included, along with their various afterwords and prefaces, as well as the closing essay 'Earthsea Revisioned', in *The Books of Earthsea: The Complete Illustrated Edition*.

'Is gender necessary? Redux' is available in *Space Crone*, Silver Press's collection of Le Guin's essays on feminisms and anarchism (and, in part, on T-shirts by Frank Duffy). *Steering the Craft* is also available from Silver Press.

The Left Hand of Darkness, *The Dispossessed*, *Always Coming Home* and *The Word for World is Forest* are all available in SF Masterworks editions.

'Coming of age in Karhide' was published in *The Birthday of the World and Other Stories*.

'The day before the revolution' and 'The ones who walk away from Omelas' were published in *The Wind's Twelve Quarters*. 'Omelas' has been widely republished. 'The Nna Mmoy language' was published in *Changing Planes*.

'Science fiction and Mrs Brown (1975)' is included in *The Language of the Night: Essays on Fantasy and Science Fiction*.

'A non-Euclidean view of California as a cold place to be' and 'Indian Uncles' are included in *Dreams Must Explain Themselves: The Selected Non-Fiction of Ursula K. Le Guin*.

Le Guin's article 'My appointment with the Enterprise: an appreciation', appeared in a *Star Trek: The Next Generation* collectors' edition of *TV Guide*, 14–20 May 1994. 'Worf (Michael Dorn)', she writes there, 'was my first love. That voice, Richter 6.5 – that forehead – those dark, worried eyes – those ethical problems!', thus demonstrating that language's power can only explained by the sappy-for-Worf hypothesis.